C000110206

Anxiety in Relationship

How to Feel Safe by Uncovering the Blocks That Prevent You from a Loving Union. Discover the Secrets of a Better Communication to Avoid Conflicts in The Couple

By
Olivia Sans

The information herein is offered for informational purposes solely, and is universal as so. The presentation of the information is without contract or any type of guarantee assurance.

The trademarks that are used are without any consent, and the publication of the trademark is without permission or backing by the trademark owner. All trademarks and brands within this book are for clarifying purposes only and are the owned by the owners themselves, not affiliated with this document.

Introduction

It is easy to produce repeated, frustrating answers to the flaws of your spouse and loses sight of how important continuity is in the overall picture of your partnership. You can turn down the influence of your emotional reactions, feel more sensitivity and think about practical methods to minimize the effects of your disputes as you step back and pursue guidance. This is not a one-and-done activity but one that you may need to frequently revisit if you see frustration or resentment rising up in a mostly successful partnership.

Emotions and actions may be affected by anxiety, and it is sometimes difficult to make anxiety go away. But note that, even when you feel caught up in anxiety, relief is possible.

Relationships can be one of the most satisfying experiences on earth. Yet they may also be a breeding ground for fears and critical thoughts. Anxiety about partnerships may arise at nearly every romantic stage. For some individuals, merely dreaming of being in a relationship can increase tensions. The early stages will have persistent worries for us. If and when people start dating: early steps will trigger a lot of problems. "Does he/she still like me?" "Can it all work out? "What's the real thing? Unfortunately, these concerns do not tend to subside in the early stages of a romantic partnership. In particular, when things become easier between a couple, distresses will get even more intense. Thoughts run like this: "Can this work out?" Do I still like him/her? "Will we have to slow things down?" "Will he/she lose confidence in such an undertaking?" "All those questions regarding our partnerships will make us feel pretty lonely. This can give us a justification to remain apart from our mate. Fear at its peak might even push one to give up completely on passion. Knowing all about the origins and effects of intimacy vulnerability can help us grasp the negative attitudes and actions that can disrupt our love lives. Why do we maintain hold of our anxiety and remain open to everyone we love?

The worries that anxious males and females have are often intensified in the relationship. Owing to their exposure to family, close associates, or others surrounding them, the usual anxiety that those with an anxiety disorder feel every day may be amplified.

Among other variables, it is often really critical to consider anxiety disorders in relationships, and it may be the key to sustaining a bond with an anxiety-focused spouse.

This book will introduce the reader to all aspects of fear and address certain reasons dependent on partnerships.

This book is intended both for the insecure person's spouse or companion and for the individual actually engaging in a relationship with anxiety.

This book explores all facets of life management while holding the anxieties and insecurities under balance. It helps people to consider their feelings and to view it from a different viewpoint. It would also help to enhance a certain ability set that will enable relationship conflicts to be handled in a far better manner rather than distancing the spouse and guessing everything all the time.

Chapter 1: General Preface on Anxiety

Anxiety disorders arise when an individual experiences excessive amounts of distress, concern, or terror about an emotional stimulus on a daily basis. Identifying the cause that raises the issue will be the

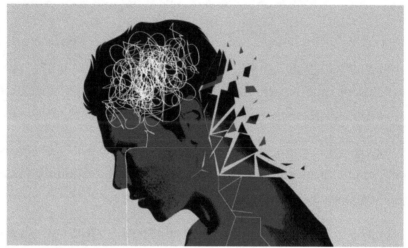

secret to effective recovery.

To aid in the assessment, the problems under the category of anxiety disorders have specific characteristics that differentiate them from regular anxiety feelings. A broad range of factors can lead to anxiety disorders.

1.1 Causes of Anxiety

Anxiety problems have a complex causal network, including:

• Environmental factors: Environmental elements may raise anxiety around a person. Pressure from a personal relationship, work, education, or financial situation may significantly lead to anxiety disorders. Also, low amounts of oxygen in high altitude environments may contribute to the effects of anxiety.

• Genetics: Those with an anxiety problem close relatives are far more likely to get one by themselves.

• Medical factors: Several medical issues can contribute to an anxiety disorder, such as drug side effects, illness complications, or tension from a specific underlying medical problem that may not specifically cause shifts in anxiety disorder, but can result in serious behavioral modifications, discomfort, or restricted motion.

• Brain chemistry: traumatic or stressful events and genetic factors can change the shape and function of the brain to respond more vigorously to stimuli that have not triggered anxiety prior. Many moods or anxiety problems are characterized by psychologists & neurologists as disturbances of chemicals and electrical signals inside the brain.

• Usage or abstinence from an addictive substance: day-to-day discomfort associated with all of the above may be a primary factor in an anxiety condition.

Often the consequence of a third person, such as a boss or spouse, is traumatic situations. However, nervous emotions can come from people convincing themselves bad things will happen. An anxiety disorder has the ability to expand without any environmental stimulation.

A mixture of one or both of the above triggers may result in excessive anxiety.

For instance, an individual may react to stress in the workplace by consuming more alcohol or taking illegal drugs, raising levels of anxiety and causing more complications.

1.2 Anxiety Disorders

Generalized anxiety disorder: This is a persistent condition that causes severe, long-lasting distress and fears over non-specific life activities, things, and circumstances. GAD is the most prevalent anxiety condition, and the origin of their fear is not necessarily known by those with the disease.

Panic disorder: The panic condition is defined by short or unexpected episodes of extreme fear and anxiety. Such attacks can cause sweating, anxiety, dizziness, nausea and difficulty in breathing. Panic attacks appear to take place and intensify quickly, peaking in 10 minutes. A panic attack could linger for hours, though.

Panic symptoms typically arise following traumatic events or excessive tension, but without a cause may also arise. A person that has a panic disorder may view it as a life-threatening condition and can make dramatic behavioral adjustments to prevent possible attacks.

Unique phobia: This is an unreasonable apprehension and avoidance of an event or a specific circumstance. Phobias aren't like most psychological conditions, since they refer to a common source.

An individual with a phobia may understand fear as illogical or severe but may not be able to regulate feelings of anxiety around the cause. The reasons for a phobia vary from daily things to circumstances and animals.

Agoraphobia: This is a fear and avoidance of locations, activities, or circumstances from which it would be impossible to flee, or that support will not be possible if an individual were stuck in. People sometimes misinterpret this disorder as a phobia of outside and open spaces, but it isn't that easy. An individual suffering from agoraphobia can be unable to leave home or use elevators and public transport.

Selective mutism: This is a type of fear exhibited by certain adolescents, in which they cannot communicate in some locations or situations, such as school, even if they might have outstanding speaking skills with familiar people. It may be a type of severe social phobia.

Social anxiety problem, or social phobia: it is a perception of other people's unfavorable judgments in certain settings or public humiliation. Social anxiety disorder involves a number of emotions, such as situation terror, trust apprehension, and worry over embarrassment and rejection.

This condition will contribute to individuals avoiding public

interactions and personal interaction to the extent that daily life is made incredibly difficult.

Separation anxiety disorder: extreme amounts of anxiety characterize separation anxiety disorder after separation from an individual or position, which provides feelings of comfort or protection. Separation may sometimes contribute to signs of fear.

1.3 Signs and Symptoms of Anxiety
Too much worry

Excessive preoccupation is one of the most prominent signs of an anxiety condition.

The wondering linked with anxiety disorders is excessive to the activities that cause it and usually happen in reaction to usual, ordinary circumstances.

To be recognized as a symptom of generalized anxiety illness, the worrying need to continue for at least six months on most days and be hard to manage.

Even the worrying has to be serious and distracting, rendering it impossible to focus and execute everyday activities.

People below the age of 65 are at the greatest risk of generalized anxiety disorder, particularly individuals with a lower socioeconomic status with several life stressors

Feeling agitated

A portion of their sympathetic nervous system goes into overdrive when someone is worried.

This sets off a series of body wide results, including a speeding heart, sweating eyes, shaking hands and dry mouth.

These symptoms arise when your brain assumes you've encountered risk and trains your body to adapt to the challenge.

In case you decide to sprint or fight, your body diverts blood away from your digestive system and into your muscles. It also raises your heart rate and allows your senses to be sharper.

While in the case of real danger, these consequences may be beneficial, they may be crippling if the anxiety is just in mind.

Some studies also show that people with anxiety disorders cannot decrease their intensity as easily as people without anxiety disorders, suggesting that they can experience the symptoms of anxiety over a longer period of time

Restlessness

Other common symptoms of anxiety are restlessness, particularly in children and teens.

They also describe it as feeling "on alert" or possessing an "uncomfortable desire to move," while they are experiencing restlessness.

One analysis of 128 children living with anxiety disorders showed that 74 percent mentioned restlessness as one of their primary signs of distress.

While not all individuals with anxiety feel restlessness, it's one of the warning signs physicians always search for before developing a diagnosis.

If you feel restlessness for longer than six months on the majority of days, this may be a symptom of an emotional condition.

Fatigue

Another possible sign of a generalized anxiety disorder is being quickly fatigued.

Some may find this condition alarming because anxiety is usually correlated with hyperactivity or enthusiasm.

Tiredness can accompany an anxiety disorder for others, whereas tiredness may be persistent for others.

If this exhaustion is attributable to other typical anxiety symptoms, such as insomnia or muscle stiffness, or if it could be linked to recurrent anxiety's hormonal consequences is unknown.

It is necessary to remember, however, that exhaustion may often be a symptom of depression or other medical problems, so exhaustion alone may not serve to diagnosis an anxiety disorder

Concentrating issues

Some individuals with anxiety experience having problems focusing.

One research of 157 children and teenagers with severe anxiety disorder showed that attention was challenging for more than two-thirds.

Another research of the same condition in 175 individuals showed that almost 90 percent were having trouble focusing. The more anxiety they had, the greater their issue was.

Some experiments suggest that fear can disrupt the working memory, a sort of memory that is responsible for retaining knowledge for the short term. This may better understand the drastic drop in results that people frequently encounter during times of significant distress.

However, cognitive problems may often be a sign of other psychiatric issues, such as attention deficit disorder or depression, so the evaluation is not adequate verification of an anxiety disorder.

Reliability

Even most individuals with anxiety problems have extreme irritability.

About 90 percent of people with generalized anxiety disorder documented becoming particularly irritable at times where their anxiety condition was at its highest, according to one new survey of more than 6,000 adults.

Young and middle-aged people with a generalized anxiety disorder showed more than twice as much irritability in their everyday lives relative to self-reporting problems.

It is no wonder the irritability is indeed a frequent symptom, considering that anxiety has been correlated with elevated arousal and unnecessary concern.

Tighten muscles

Using tensed muscles is another common sign of fear on certain periods of a week.

Although tense muscles can be normal, why they're correlated with anxiety, it is not confirmed.

It is likely because muscle tension itself causes symptoms of anxiety, and it is also probable that anxiety contributes to elevated muscle tension, or both are triggered by a third component.

Interestingly, managing body stress through muscle relaxation treatment in people with a generalized anxiety disorder has been found to alleviate fear. Some reports also suggest that cognitive behavioral counseling is as successful as

Trouble dropping or dreaming

Anxiety conditions are closely correlated with sleep disruptions.

The two most often recorded concerns are getting up in the dark of night and experiencing difficulty falling asleep.

Some evidence shows that experiencing insomnia during adolescence may also be correlated with anxiety occurring later in life.

A survey of almost 1,000 children up to the age of 20 showed that childhood insomnia was correlated with a 60 percent elevated chance of experiencing an anxiety problem until age 26.

Although insomnia and anxiety are closely related, it is unknown whether insomnia leads to anxiety, or anxiety leads to insomnia or both.

Something is understood is that insomnia frequently improves even when the associated anxiety condition is handled

Panic attacks

Repetitive panic disorders are correlated with one form of anxiety condition called panic condition.

Panic attacks generate an extreme, debilitating feeling of terror and can collapse.

Usually, this intense anxiety is followed by fast pounding, sweating, trembling, and chest tightness, difficulty in breathing, nausea & fear of death or losing power.

Panic attacks may appear in isolation, but they may be a symptom of panic disorder if they arise regularly and suddenly.

An approximate 22% of adults aged may have a panic condition at any stage in their life, but just around 3% encounter it intensely enough to satisfy the panic disorder criterion

Evitable Social Conditions

If you notice yourself: You can display symptoms of social anxiety condition.

• feeling insecure or frightened about social situations to come

• Worried that others might judge you or examine you

• Fearful of embarrassing or humiliating others

• Due to various suspicions, avoid those social activities

Social anxiety is very widespread, impacting somewhere in their lifetime, about 12 percent of American adolescents.

Social anxiety, in adulthood, continues to grow early. In reality, around 50% of those that have it are infected with age 11, whereas age 20 diagnoses 80%.

Individuals having social anxiety can seem in groups to be excessively shy and silent, or while meeting other people. Though on the exterior, they do not look distraught, they experience intense anxiety and fear inside.

This gap may also trigger individuals experiencing social anxiety to look snobbish or unapproachable, but the condition is correlated with such as low self-esteem, strong self-criticism & depression.

Irrational Fears

Strong anxiety of certain objects like insects, confined spaces or elevations may be a result of a phobia.

A phobia is characterized as intense anxiety or terror about a particular item or circumstance. The discomfort is serious enough to mess with the capacity of regular work.

Some typical phobias consist of:

• Animal phobia: Dislike of individual species or insects

• Environmental Phobias: Terror of extreme disasters such as storms or flooding

• Phobias blood-injection-accident: blood-fear, injection, needle or accident

• Scenario phobias: Terrified in such circumstances, such as planes or elevator trips

Agoraphobia is yet another phobia causing apprehension of two or three of just the following:

• The use of public transportation

• Reside in open areas

• Living in tight areas

• queue up or be in lines

• Being isolated outside the house

For any stage in their life, phobias impact 12.5 percent of Americans. They appear to evolve in infancy or adolescence and are much more prevalent in females than males

1.4 Is Anxiety Chronic?

GAD is indeed a long-term disorder that makes people feel nervous over a wide variety of circumstances and problems, rather than just one single incident.

Individuals with GAD are often nervous and frequently fail to recall the very last occasion they looked comfortable.

If one nervous thinking has been resolved, another can occur over another question.

Generalized Anxiety Disorder (GAD) signs

GAD may induce both physical (mental) as well as psychological symptoms.

These vary by person, but may include:

• Sensation of restlessness or fear

- Hard to relax or to sleep

- Heart palpitations or dizziness

What Induces Generalized Disease of Anxiety (GAD)?

The precise trigger for GAD remains not well known, but a mixture of many variables is likely to play a part.

Analysis has indicated this may include:

- Over-activity of brain regions influenced by feelings and actions

- Deficiency of the brain substances nor-adrenaline and serotonin implicated in emotion modulation and management

- The genes you receive from your ancestors-if you have a family member with the disorder, you are predicted to be fivefold more prone to acquire GAD

- Have a history of encounters of tension or pain, such as domestic assault, child neglect or bullying

- Include long-term debilitating health problems, like arthritis

- Has a background of alcohol or substance abuse

But for no specific cause, many people still grow GAD.

Who Is Impacted

GAD is a chronic disease and is projected to impact up to 5 % of the population in the UK.

It affects far more females than males, and the disorder is more prevalent in people aged 35 to 59.

How to Treat Generalized Anxiety Disorder (GAD)

GAD can impact your everyday life greatly, although there are many alternative medications available that will relieve the symptoms.

Including:

• Psychological interventions – psychological treatments such as cognitive-behavioral therapy (CBT) will be accessed through the NHS; you do not require a GP referral because you may apply to psychological counseling facilities throughout your region

• Medication – such as the antidepressant form known as (SSRI)

A number of people are able to manage their fear levels through medication. Yet, for a long time, certain therapies may need to be done, and there may be times where the conditions become worse.

Generalized Anxiety Disorder (GAD) self-help

There are still plenty of items you should do to further minimize the fear, like:

• Heading through a path in self-help

• Running occasionally

• Quit smoking

• Reduce the volume of alcohol and caffeine you are consuming

Chapter 2: Anxiety and Relationship

Working into your friendship requires more than just love.

While love is really the cornerstone of every good intimate partnership, love isn't enough. All partners must be able to compromise on it in hopes of maintaining a good partnership. Below are tips for maintaining your partnership.

2.1 What You Must Know To Sustain a Great Relationship

Learn recognition and respect. Acceptance and gratitude are two doors to a conscientious relationship. We are there knowingly, non-intrusively, in a real friendship with you-and-I, the way we are there with items in existence. We may not suggest it should be anything of an elm than a birch tree. We may not have a purpose; we just enjoy it.

Only choose the term "we" Couples that use the term "we" while communicating are healthier, calmer and happier with their partnerships in general than couples whose dialogue is more dominated by the pronouns "you," "me," and "I."

A big change is the term "we." It kicks off a communication mechanism inside the brain such that we are in a competitive mentality rather than being in an attitude of "me vs. you." This collective mentality is making us more compassionate and caring.

Realize that both relations have their highs and lows. Just like you can't promise to be satisfied all of the time, you ought not to anticipate your relationship being at an ever peak. You have to be able to enjoy the peaks together, and also the downs, as you create a long-lasting commitment to another.

Ignore the schedule of appreciation for three days. Rita Watson, an associate colleague at Yale's Ezra Stiles Program, describes that the romantic life can be revitalized with a mindset of appreciation. Watson suggests that a survey involving 77 wedded heterosexual as well as monogamous couples noticed that "participants indicated becoming more affectionate with conveyed appreciation."

"They started being more relaxed, more entertained and more proud too. They viewed their companion as being much more compassionate, more validating, more supportive and more sensitive in general. They were much more likely to have recorded thanking their companion unexpectedly for anything they would enjoy on any specific day. And they became more pleased with the overall nature of their partnership.'

To continue by adding more appreciation into your partnership, she proposes that below three-day thanking plan:

• Day 1: Discover the three things you enjoy in your mate and spend every day on such three attributes.

• Day 2: Define three items about your companion that infuriate you. Now excuse them for this matter.

• Day 3: Say only positive terms to your beloved other for the whole day.

Think about the three-day strategy as a detox that helps you to remove your emotions from flourishing.

Retain the novelties active. One of the good benefits of being in a serious relationship with someone is that you are both getting to know each other. The other side of this is the novelty is fading off, and people enjoy novelty.

There is also a way to hold the fun alive: pursue different things together continuously. This causes the suspense and confusion that comes from the unexpected; regardless, you know someone like the back of your hand.

Hold the ratio 3:1. We provide an abundance of good and unpleasant interactions over the span of a day. This also holds valid when it falls to our partnership with our other significant. Many people believe all is good so far as the pleasant interactions surpass the bad. But this is not true. It's the positive-negative ratio that counts.

Analysis has found that for a thriving relationship, the perfect ratio is 3:1 or better. That is, to maintain a good friendship, you have to have three times more supportive interactions with your spouse than painful ones.

Preserve the playfulness. We just love to play, no matter how old we might be. Do the following: have fun together; bring together something ridiculous, and just let go. Also, the next time your partner does something that upsets you, aim to react with a smile rather than being angry.

Give space to your partner. Using porcupines, the philosopher Arthur Schopenhauer clarified a problem that sometimes occurs in human affairs. Two porcupines will travel closer to each other, seeking to stay warm. They poke one another with their spines, though if they get too tight.

In human partnerships, this very same thing occurs: we want closeness, but we also want the room. The trick is reaching the sweet spot where we experience the love that emerges from being in a partnership, but at the same time enabling each person to have enough room such that no one behaves like they're being pinched by the spines of each other (feelings of missing autonomy, feeling cramped, etc.).

Using AAA. Mira Kirshenbaum, a psychotherapist and creator of "The Weekend Union," describes why you should use the AAA method anytime your significant other is angry over what you have achieved. This is an explanation, an attraction and a pledge of intervention. To explain:

• Talk to your companion that you are sorry you harmed or upset them.

• Deliver a positive warming touch, for example, an embrace or kiss.

• Promise that they will take an initiative that is positive.

Display deep love for one another every day. Studies show a wide variety of benefits of physical love. It produces feel-good emotions, lowers blood pressure, helps relieve stress, improves morale, and is linked to greater satisfaction in the relationship.

It may be as natural to display mutual intimacy as embracing, locking hands, smiling, offering a back scratch or wrapping a hand on the other person's arm.

The Constructive Outlook. Since 1986 Dr. Terri Orbit has undertaken a long-term analysis of what keeps partners satisfied and improves partnerships. She says couples are willing to reflect on the better. She states why successful couples are centered on what goes right with their partnership, rather than on what goes wrong.

Furthermore, if you choose to draw attention to a bad factor, strive to do so favorably. When your partner is dirty, for example, consider asking them something like this: "It makes me so happy to come home to a clean house. I get depressed when things get wrong. Let's come up with a plan.'

Withdraw critics. Partners who stop expressing some rational thinking that falls into their minds while addressing touchy subjects are often the happier ones.

Establish routines for partners. You can improve the partnership by establishing routines only between you two. Any Saturday night, for instance, can be a dinner date. Another idea may be to get your coffee together every morning or to talk every night before heading to bed for ten minutes.

Be compassionate. There are several forms the companion should be helped, including:

• Offer them emotional support: listen when they're sad, and they need to chat.

• Give support and complement.

• Share possibly needed facts.

• Offer a helping hand in times of need. For, e.g., because they decide to put in extra hours at work, you can do their house chores.

Show "I love you" with actions. Carry out little acts of compassion with your companion and let them know you value them. There are some ideas which include:

• Make a cup of coffee in the morning for her.

• bring food from his favorite Chinese restaurant.

• Wake up fifteen minutes before she wakes up so that when she heads into the kitchen, breakfast is set.

• A little fun present for him while you're out shopping.

Let yourself be soft. The secret to relational connection is openness. She continues that honesty is about being truthful about how we felt, our worries, what we require and what we need to wish for. It helps us to be genuinely accepted by our friends, warts and all else.

Combat fairly. Relationships are not broken by conflicts but by how you cope with them.

We are sure to have differences. The question is, are you going into it in a spirit of striving for peace or are you going into it in a spirit of having even, revenge, and power? If you do that, you can never win. If you're making your relationship a contest that implies your partner has to lose for you to win. It is not a contest; it is a partnership.'

Some of the strategies for fair combat are as follows:

• Realize what you're attempting to achieve.

• Set limits around the conversation, so you don't wind up fighting about any bad thing that's ever occurred in your partnership.

• Evite assassination of characters.

• Effective listening training. Try and paraphrase and make sure you hear what the other individual was thinking and inquire for clarity if there is anything you are not certain on.

• Set deadline.

• develop an Ability to negotiate.

• Have a consensus on how you'll fix the issue.

Set targets as a team. Be a two-person team that aims to fulfill a series of targets that you have established together and that are essential to each of you. You'll accomplish all of the above by establishing targets together:

• You are trying to make sure you're still headed in the same direction.

• The losses are the gains.

• Every time you hit a landmark, you should rejoice together.

Studies have found that one of the essential aspects of success is to aim for objectives you feel significant to accomplish. One part of a good partnership, in particular, is to have a collection of aspirations that you are seeking to accomplish together.

2.2 Understanding Negative Attraction

The bad attraction is more common than you acknowledge.

If you don't get what you desire, even though you're striving to pursue and create a happier existence, you're definitely experiencing a detrimental attraction. This is where you begin to draw bad circumstances, even more than you like

No matter what you do, it feels like nothing is effective. Only because you've got detrimental attraction.

You still don't know that you've got detrimental attraction, and you're curious how it all happened? You want a brighter future, after all, you want to win, you want to earn more money and fulfill your dream, but nothing seems to fit.

The bad attraction is something that you have been cultivating over time. Of course, you and millions of others are not purposely creating toxic attraction.

You end up with detrimental appeal because the attention is not attuned to what you really want.

Bad attraction occurs because you have more detrimental energies than optimistic.

Then you have bad energies causing unpleasant conditions.

No matter what you do, nothing is changing, and it is not going to.

You wind up with all of what you don't like, all of the unpleasant circumstances and things just tend to go from poor to worse.

You may continue and remember and be optimistic, but nothing you do can succeed if you have so much bad energy. You are probably not going to be able to move ahead.

It's all that the toxic energy inhibits your potential; it's preventing you and keeping your subconscious mind from pursuing you and doing what you want in your life.

This emotional attitude is the product of previous bad thoughts and false perceptions that suggest you can't achieve anything or that something is impossible to accomplish. Poor thought and pessimistic attitudes discourage you from taking even the very first move toward your target.

And I do agree; we all have those pessimistic feelings.

Yet negative energy is entirely different, and until you take a deeper look, you may not really know you have negative energy.

What is your energy? Bad or Constructive

Here's how to figure out what the amount of energy is and where it's going. Only answer the following questions, and be honest:

If you think you're having trouble doing what you desire or succeed?

Do you think getting more wealth is hard?

Do you have problems sleeping through the night?

Do you think about the future, or get stressed?

Think you've had to struggle hard to get ahead?

You just don't see yourself with enough time?

Led with the financial challenges?

You would have some bad feelings if you responded yes to all of these issues.

The more yes replies, you've got the more bad thoughts.

Saying yes to all of the above is a strong indication that you are producing toxic energies, and this is likely to contribute to more stress in your life.

The tougher life is as you find more disappointment.

That's how you put the bad energies out there.

And the bad energy can create more stressful conditions that can only exacerbate existence.

For example: if you assume and feel that it is impossible to achieve or accomplish what you desire, then you can encounter the circumstances, people and resources that make it challenging for you to accomplish.

If you assume and feel that making more money or finding the right person is impossible, so you can still encounter circumstances, individuals and resources that make it challenging for you to find the right partner or earn more profits.

So whatever you think and feel is what forms your subconscious mind. That's how your subconscious only makes sure your life is a representation of what you think and feel.

You would then move from having harmful energy of attraction to getting positive energy of attraction so that your subconscious mind gets you what you desire.

You do that by modifying what you perceive and feel.

So if you think it's difficult to do anything, then you have to adjust certain thoughts to build ideas and opinions that more conveniently lead to what you want

Only trying to imagine that making money is easy isn't going to work effectively.

It's because you've got all these negative stories, negative feelings, and pessimistic attitudes that suggest money-making is hard.

So if you only think it's simple, you're just going to get enormous resistance from your brain, and you're going to give up.

Instead, you would worry about why you can excel, how you can do what you desire, when and how you can accomplish what you want.

You have to re-program the way you feel and perceive.

You must establish different ways of thought and belief so you can transfer the focus from inside.

Then you would be generating positive energies and drawing individuals, circumstances and chances to be good.

You're going to allow your forces to function for you to get what you want. You will remove the influence of harmful attraction.

The world and others are sucking up the room.

Based on your personality, they react to you, and your subconscious mind brings others into your existence who complement your intensity.

Positive thinking creates good souls, optimistic outcomes and contributes to a pleasant and healthy life.

Bad behavior draws individuals who are cynical, bad circumstances that contribute to unpleasant lives.

Eliminate Toxic Energy

Your body is comprised of your convictions and emotions.

Your subconscious mind is taking information from your emotions and values.

And it constructs your life around what you think and feel.

When you have optimistic thinking and values, you're going to draw good individuals, optimistic circumstances, and you're

going to have a happy existence where things work for you.

When you have pessimistic feelings and negative views, you are going to draw bad individuals, negative circumstances, and you are going to live a miserable existence where things don't work for you.

Get rid of your underlying pessimistic feelings and opinions, and you'll also shift your attitude from pessimistic to constructive.

Your subconscious mind can associate you with more optimistic individuals, giving you more productive scenarios, meaning you can achieve what you want faster.

You just need to give them the correct guidance.

You just need to rid yourself of the destructive thoughts and perceptions that rest on your subconscious and obstruct your progress.

Only adjusting what's in your mind.

You are a good guy.

You have immense power.

Now start to work with your strength.

Your subconscious mind is the force

You can generate good energy and get it.

Then you are going to gain and get more of what you desire, and you are going to get rid of the bad energy that has been holding you for long.

Start generating the optimistic energy today – take responsibility for your consciousness and subconscious mind now

How do your partnerships get affected by your anxiety?

Based on the symptoms you encounter, anxiety can affect your relationships in a variety of different ways. For others, it can lead them to excessively rely on their family members while others may remove themselves for fear of humiliation or being a burden.

We also go into some of the typical forms the partnerships are impacted by the general anxiety disorder.

Anxiety is the reverse of acceptance.

A safe type of concern can warn you that "something is wrong;" it occurs from a fast tug to your heart or a tense feeling in your stomach. This signal encourages you to respond, especially when you stand up about someone who is being unfairly served.

Unhealthy anxiety levels render you feel like an emotional "stone" is almost continuously in your stomach. Anxiety leads you to ignore non-hazardous items and stop things that would help you. It may even discourage you from taking positive steps to improve problems that affect you in your life, so it makes you feel helpless or trapped.

Because it's awkward training, you don't have to dismiss an awkward idea or worry. If possible, take constructive action. Occasionally your spouse just needs you to be evident with their feelings, and sometimes you have to offer yourself the same gift. With gentle eyes or a light touch, you can demonstrate your existence to your companion and be available with a soothing breath.

Being too reliant

Anxiety may also lead an entity to become too reliant. Their fear may render them worried about being alone or coping with such things on their own. Anxiety may also trigger an individual to doubt any choice they make, which may contribute to over-dependence as well.

Because of this, anyone with anxiety may have a strong need to remain near to their friends, relatives, or wife and maybe searching for continuous reassurance and encouragement.

This overreliance can trigger social experiences to overthink, causing them to worry about others not reacting quickly via telephone or social networking.

People who rely excessively on their relationships can struggle with effective communication and strike out in ways that are detrimental to their ties. This might physically and mentally lead friends and family to maintain their distance.

Anxiety takes away pleasure from you.

Experiencing joy calls for a feeling of comfort or independence. Anxiety makes us feel either terrified or impaired. A brain and body conditioned to cope will therefore have a much tougher time loving love and sex. Negative feelings and worries have an effect on the willingness of an individual to be involved within a friendship and ultimately drain the fun out of a moment.

Consider not yourself too seriously, though. To combat fear, you should use your sense of humor. Try and make your buddy chuckle and play. Joy strengthens and comforts the brain emotionally in ways that are essential to a stable partnership.

Individual solitary imprisonment

On the other side, certain insecure individuals separate themselves and quit interactions so as to prevent bad emotions (like being upset or irritated with a mate or loved one).

It may be daunting to open up to others you are nearest to and be friendly to. Because of that, although you are striving for closeness, others may view you as distant, stand-off or emotionally inaccessible, which makes it incredibly difficult, and often impossible, to preserve and establish new ties.

Trust and communication are taken down by anxiety

Anxiety triggers concern or stress, and in a given moment, can render you less conscious of your true needs. It may even leave you less attuned to your partner's needs. If you're concerned about what might happen, it's hard to pay attention to what's going on. If you're frustrated, your spouse can feel like you're not there.

This way, teach the brain to survive at the moment. Stop to reflect on what you do know (as compared to what you don't know) whether you encounter insecurity or anxiety that triggers your mind to wander from the truth or the current moment. Before you actually behave, slow down. You should take purposeful measures to develop trust within your relationship. Speak freely when you feel nervous, and intentionally reach out (physically or verbally) to your spouse when you would usually retreat or strike in panic.

Chronic Tension

Those who are nervous often feel stressed or irritated, and those around them may sense the discomfort. If someone has anxiety, others sometimes don't know how to react to it and may feel like they need to navigate around that individual on eggshells.

This stress can trigger interaction issues and communication problems in relationships.

Anxiety is suppressing the true speech, generating fear or procrastination.

Anyone who appears to be nervous may have difficulty voicing their true emotions. Maintaining fair limits when demanding for the consideration or room required may often be challenging.

Since feeling fear is stressful, you can subconsciously plan to delay their encounter. On the other side, fear may lead you to feel that something has to be spoken about instantly, while a slight break can potentially be helpful.

If you don't articulate what you actually want or need, so fear grows worse. And, if you leave them in, the emotions will inevitably spin off balance. You might get frustrated and defensive.

... But let the emotions be known earlier rather than later. For it to be handled, a thought or fear should not be a tragedy. Approach your companion with empathy, because you're not panicking nor procrastinating. Find time to unpack any of the emotions or worries that linger through your head, too; they rob your attention and resources.

Anxiety leads to greedy actions.

Since anxiety is an overactive reaction to fear, often, anyone who experiences it can concentrate very strongly on their own worries or issues.

Your expectations and fears can bring undue pressure to bear on your relationship. You might like you need to care about defending yourself in your partnership, but maybe that may prevent you from being caring and open to your spouse.

If your wife has anxiety, you can sometimes build up anger and respond in selfish ways. The behaviors we hold and the experiences are infectious. It is extremely difficult to hold the stress levels under check while the partner is feeling nervous, angry or defensive.

Please take control of your wants and not your concerns. Take a minute to remember the love you have towards yourself and your family, as you find yourself being afraid or protective. Demand specifically the help you need to be supported and heard. Excuse yourself for allowing fear to get you self-absorbed.

2.3 Recognizing what Triggers the Anxiety

Anxiety-dealing individuals may doubt how to classify causes for anxiety. While each person has specific causes of anxiety, there are several common factors among anxious people. Identifying anxiety causes can help a person develop the correct coping mechanisms to better handle their illness.

Recognition strategies for anxiety causes include:

• Keep a journal: Keep track of your thoughts on paper as it's a nice tool to help you understand circumstances that render you nervous. Additionally, writing down some successful coping mechanisms can be valuable for potential reference.

• Recognize big stressors: life stressors such as interpersonal complications, career shifts or losses, pregnancy, or a loved one's death may all contribute to anxiety; Think of any recent stressors that could trigger the degree of anxiety right now.

• Focus on prior experiences: Fear may be caused by recent stress. Taking the time to remember how traumatic events from the past might even impact you now.

• Speak to someone: A trustworthy acquaintance or family member may offer useful input into circumstances that cause anxiety. Try seeking a licensed trainer to help you move with the causes if you require extra assistance.

• Listen to the body: Take care of what you consume. Caffeine, processed drinks, and alcohol may all escalate levels of cortisol that can raise anxiety.

Identifying causes of anxiety takes much time and resources but may enable a person to learn the appropriate coping mechanisms to control his illness. When causes for anxiety are established, a person can learn how to deal with them.

Chapter 3: Insecurity

It can be extremely difficult and disturbing to feel uncomfortable about your relationship. It can appear in all sorts of forms. You may think like your partner is often going to split up with you. You may have problems believing them not to rat on you. Or you may think like the bond has gotten progressively weaker for some time, and that the pillars are starting to slip apart.

3.1 How to Stop Feeling Insecure in a Relationship

Feeling like this will make things very challenging to maintain a great deal of confidence in your future, together-which can even have you questioning if breaking up will be the best option. Even it may start causing very detrimental consequences in other aspects of your existence. It will weaken your self-esteem and trust, and this will make it impossible to be ready to resolve some concerns.

From where does insecurity originate?

A feeling of insecurity may originate from a variety of different positions in your relationship.

If you and your spouse have not been actively talking about problems or making an attempt to preserve your bond, you may start feeling as though you are falling apart.

Insecurity may also be a result of shifts in the relationship. For e.g., whether you have moved in together or married recently, you may experience all sorts of different stresses and pressures. If you can't resolve this together, so you can start getting less positive in your abilities to function as a team.

It may even arise from self-image or self-esteem problems. For example, if you felt especially depressed after having taken on weight following a number of disappointments in your professional life or less satisfied with your physical image, this might cause you to worry about your relationship.

Often we will bring emotions from previous relationships into our new partnership-even those with family members. If we weren't getting very stable or caring partnerships when we were younger with our parents or primary caregivers, we might be taking the feeling with us as adults. Past intimate relationships where the faith has been violated will make it hard to faith someone else. You can catch yourself checking for 'patterns' or thinking history would replicate itself.

What to do to combat insecurity?

The first contact is to discuss it through together. This can be complicated, of course-particularly if you haven't been communicating properly for a while or you feel upset or frustrated with your partner.

If you do feel competent, however, you may find the following tips helpful:

• Keep yourself calm. Hearing the words 'we must speak' will cause a protective feeling even for the most laid back individual! The more optimistic presentation of situations will bring us off to a stronger start. You might want to say something like, 'I really would like to speak to you about our relationship when you have a chance.'

• Pick the time you desire. Start interacting while things go right and not poorly. Putting it up in the midst of a dispute will only generate more tension. If you raise the issue when you feel comfortable about the partnership, both of you are more inclined to step in a constructive direction.

• Say how you felt, not how you think they're making you act. When all of you are just throwing blows and accusing each other of anything, you certainly won't go anywhere. To hold things under check, it would be helpful to use phrases about 'I' ('I still feel worried about that') rather than phrases about 'you' ('you still make me feel worried because').

• Listen. Even if it's uncomfortable to know what your companion has to suggest, aim to stay with it. For it to succeed, a dialogue has to go both directions. Help to begin by understanding their viewpoint may be different from yours.

• You might plan. It might seem a little vague, but it might be helpful to think about what you want to tell in advance. That doesn't involve making up a laundry list of complaints, but actually compiling your opinions on what you want to chat on.

• Come back to it. Rarely in one conversation are these problems fixed. Working on relationship problems requires time and commitment, but you will decide to discuss it after a month to see how you're moving on with each other. This kind of talk would sound much less disgusting after a bit!

3.2 How to Be More Confident – A Step by Step Process For Becoming Truly Confident

So many people overestimate what they are not and neglect what they are.

It cannot be overestimated how necessary it is to learn how to be more secure in our lives.

It is, after all, a lack of trust, which causes the sway of culture to flip our lives to and fro. We see the negative impact of low trust on our decision-making process since the very beginning when fear of failure becomes an all too familiar presence in our lives. This allows us to accept community ideals and indulge in previously inappropriate behavior.

To put it plainly, the desire for affection, belonging, and recognition becomes greater than the compass inside us. And several life-threatening options are starting to arise.

This desire for recognition in puberty starts to express itself in drug misuse, underage alcohol, risky sexual activities, or devious behavior.

Some of these patterns continue as we grow older; however, new ones tend to develop. The need to gain recognition by impressing with my riches; those around me continues to inspire facets of my personality. And whether it's a certain household-size, automobile-model, clothing-trend, or state-of-the-art technology, much of our acquisitions are produced with a clear urge to catch up with the neighbors and not deemed "to slip behind."

The desire for perception and approval becomes more critical than wise patterns of expenditure.

Yet self-confidence is redirecting our lives. With the special core within us, it helps to realign our needs. It encourages one to resist the patterns of a market-oriented society. When it's present in our lives, we tend to think we exist for a reason greater than shopping on Black Friday. The urge to please others with our possessions is substituted with an intrinsic need to pursue our heart and mind, and following the needs deep inside our hearts is denying the notion of welcoming shopping.

Find some realistic suggestions to renew your life, learn how to feel more optimistic, and adopt a positive sense of self-confidence:

Avoid having distinctions. Reject the urge to equate oneself with someone. We still equate the bad stuff we recognize about ourselves against the positive aspects we recognize about ourselves as we associate ourselves with others. The eventual consequence still leaves one with emotions of insufficiency and misery. Get smarter. Say to yourself, and you may not be willing to make a reasonable analogy. And totally condemn the proposal.

Celebrate the singularity. Your life was never supposed to be played out like everyone else. You don't look the same, you don't talk the same, your strengths aren't the same, and the beliefs that you keep deep are special. Throwing it away only for the benefit of someone getting welcomed is one of the cruelest acts you will ever do. And that will always deter us from enjoying our life to the fullest. Instead, support the things that make you special and trust them.

Adjust your feelings. Concentrate less on failures and focus on optimistic ones. Avoid reflecting on previous derogatory experiences and start concentrating on the optimistic aspects of today's existence.

See previous mistakes as tools for improvement. At any point in our life, we've both tried and struggled. Confident individuals think back on the mistakes and consider them as moments of growth. In this sense, mistakes will, in turn, offer more self-confidence to go on. Learn from faults, then attempt again. Know when you fail; it isn't done; it ends when you quit.

Help out, someone. One of the most crucial moves in your life to gain self-worth is to devote oneself to others. Serving another individual almost often contributes to a positive awareness that you are valuable in this life, that you have something to give, and that your existence makes the world more amazing. See someone around you who would love a helping hand? If it's a time constraint, budgets, or a compassionate mind, fulfill it today. And the life you are altering may just be your own.

Start understanding the dream of a lifetime. Intentionally and deliberately, begin to move on a purpose for existence. Know that taking the first move is a creator of momentum, which will create trust in your existence. There is a clear distinction in "I want to ..." and "I'm starting to ..." So compose the first article, run the first mile or reach the first individual. You recognize what you want to do, and you understand the first step. Avoid convincing yourself that something is out of control and undertake the first move.

Admit the limitations. Although it contributes to a loss of self-confidence to focus on our shortcomings, acknowledging them is a necessary phase in its growth. Firstly, it protects us from dangerous grandiose fantasies. It accepts that we are not flawless and keeps us in a safe desire for others to fulfill our lives. Second, it establishes the basis for us to recognize mistakes as they occur. When we fall, we are not taken off balance. Instead, we are clearly told yet again that we require someone to complement our shortcomings.

Be cherished, and be recognized. There's no greater path to self-confidence when someone else is personally identified and truly valued. One of the most important things in the world today is to invite another human being into the darkest reaches of our hearts. Although doing so (and being cherished through it) breathes vitality into our spirit and creates confidence in our innermost being and this faith tends to develop as the relationship with each other deepens.

Learning actively about how to be more optimistic can give you the inspiration to follow your interests. It offers the ground for dismissing the arguments of a consumerist society. And it gives the opportunity to pursue the life that you have always desired to enjoy.

3.3 How to Overcome Romantic Insecurity?

Let go of the requirements that you have put on yourself to merit affection.

The hidden conviction: "He can only accept me if I am such and such" is what can sometimes be found underneath intimacy insecurities as well as what further enhances self-doubt. In some stage, when you keep this conviction, you send a signal to yourself that you're not truly lovable at your essence, for who you actually are, rather that you have to merit affection by doing some stuff and acting in specific ways. We chose our partnerships, and they are the ones who choose us as well.

You need to commit to a partnership, of course, for it to be successful. To succeed, it is important to bring effort into your relationship. Its good doing lovely things for your companion, showing love and appreciation, creating morale and having them feel secure and valued. But for being the one deserving of affection, you don't need to do those stuff.

If only if we follow those standards, we feel deserving of affection, the feeling lies in a shaky field simply because we may occasionally struggle. Everyone does. Therefore it is necessary to begin to value yourself for who you truly are and not based on what you do. To know that because of who you are, your companion is with you (even though you're not clear about it at the moment). Through this, love for oneself may be extremely beneficial!

Tame the self-criticism inside you

People with a powerful inner critic realize how important it is to silence the irritating voice that brings them down. This tiny voice is so relentless and so compelling often that we embrace it as our truth.

Because sometimes it can be too noisy and so rooted in our habits of thinking, the answer is not to switch it off; it's mostly difficult. Pay heed instead of what the voice means and then consciously speak up for yourself. Handle your inner critic as a kid you're attempting to control. This method, you become conscious of your self-diminishing emotions, take a step backward and then make an active attempt to redefine them. It helps you to condemn negative views toward yourself and, as a true representation of who you are, adopt a more rational approach.

This sort of self-talk may sound a little bit awkward at the beginning like you're feigning it. Through patience, though, it typically begins to sound a little less like work, and very much like an authentic activity.

Communicate freely and efficiently with your companion

In a partnership, it is important to be honest about what you and your spouse really need and consider practical and rational approaches to support each other to satisfy them. Be mindful that this form of communication needs all participants to surrender defensiveness and stereotypes, and to be generous, truthful, and transparent to each other. An intimate relationship provides a secure atmosphere where you can function halfway to conquer insecurities and satisfy one another. This is often not straightforward, particularly if there are everlasting difficulties and tensions in a partnership, but it can be achieved with a joint effort.

It can be challenging to cope with vulnerability in a relationship since it needs you to struggle with your core values and to make an active attempt to shake the habits that have dominated your mindset for years. Nevertheless, it is achievable through discipline, self-reflection and good contact through your mate. And note, also, that it doesn't have to be a solo war. Encouragement and support from somebody you value will make things even more bearable, like a friend or a psychiatrist. Not only can learning to handle your anxieties improve the consistency of your mental wellbeing, but also the consistency of your intimate partnerships.

Create the capabilities list (temporary solution)

It would be useful to draw up a compilation of all your good qualities as an immediate lift to your self-esteem. In a partnership, this list reflects what you add to the table. Get imaginative and note down every good detail you might think about. Now is not the moment to be humble. You might have a pretty grin; maybe you're a nice kisser. You may not have a smoking 'hot body, but you are caring and sound appreciative of your spouse. Perhaps you're not that amusing, but you are reliable and a decent cook on top of that. Yeah, no one is flawless. But it's necessary to remember that being cherished doesn't need to be flawless. It is imperfections that make us unique. Learn to love the singularity.

One crucial point to bear in mind is that the motive you deserve to be cherished is not reflected by this list. It can merely act as a reminder about how many good qualities you have since they are simple to overlook during moments about heavy self-doubt. You, as a special human being, are loveable in all your habits and memories and wounds and mannerisms. Let it sink in. This is impossible to acknowledge often.

Chapter 4: Negative Thinking

As we have started exploring, negative feelings are entirely natural.

We wouldn't be around to recognize good ones without them. At the very same time, if you feel that you have a persistent inclination toward one specific emotion, particularly a negative one, it is worth considering why that could be.

4.1 How to Deal With Strong Negative Emotions

I have outlined 8 of the most prevalent negative feelings and why they can arise:

Anger

Has anybody ever ordered you not to do something you desire? What does it feel to you? Will your blood start to burn, your temperature goes up, and do you see red symbolically? This is generally how outrage is defined. Your body reacts to stuff that doesn't go your way, and it's a strategy to try to resolve it.

We also yell while we're mad, our face registers our rage, and we might even throw stuff around. In a case, we are struggling to have our own way, and that's the only approach we can think have how. It's a smart idea to discuss why and think of more constructive solutions if you're always responding to situations in this way.

Fear

As one of the main fundamental feelings, fear is frequently quoted, and that's because it's closely connected to our sense of personal-preservation. It's an emerging answer to alert us about hazardous circumstances, unpredictable challenges or shortcomings. We don't feel distressed as a result of fear; on the opposite, it's there to help us effectively handle the possible threat. You will also train yourself proactively to overcome obstacles by accepting the feeling of fear and questioning why it occurs.

Annoyance

Have you had a buddy who speaks too quickly, perhaps? Does your companion leave their messy dishes in the kitchen at all times? These habits can make people feel very irritated while we might like our friend and love our spouse. Referring to Pluchik's wheel, you will see that the lesser form of anger is irritation. Though not quite as extreme as anger, something has occurred, or somebody is doing something you feel they wouldn't. It's the product of a similar thinking process. And you don't have much say over it.

Anxiety

Anxiety tries to alert us of possible risks and hazards, just like fear. As it is believed that possessing a nervous temperament impairs judgment and our capacity to behave, it is also viewed as a detrimental emotion. The latest studies finds the contrary.

Zein, Wyatt and Grezes (2015) reported that getting anxiety improved the capacity of participants to identify faces with signs of frustration or terror. They assessed neural impulses in the brain and observed that participants who were not psychologically afflicted transferred their focus from perceptual to motor (bodily action) pathways (expressing emotion). Members with anxiety were essentially more likely to react to potential challenges and adapt.

Guilt

Guilt is a twisted emotion. We may say this for ourselves and past actions that we wish hadn't existed, but also regarding how our conduct affects others around us. Guilt is sometimes referred to as a 'positive instinct,' which can be another important mechanism for motivating us to improve our lives.

Apathy

Apathy may be a complicated feeling, similar to guilt. If you've lost your passion, inspiration, or curiosity in the stuff you've loved before, this could be due to apathy. Like anger, as we lose the influence of a circumstance or event, it may emerge; however, we seek a more silent-aggressive gesture of resistance instead of being furious.

Sadness

You'll actually feel disappointed if you miss a target, get a poor score, or don't obtain the career you've got your sights focused on. Sadness occurs whether we are disappointed with ourselves, our successes, or someone else's actions around us. Sadness may be a positive emotion since it tells us that we're enthusiastic about something. For embracing progress, it can be a perfect impetus.

Wavering

Have you ever attempted several times to complete a certain mission or objective and struggled to succeed? Does that leave you feeling like tossing your hands up in the air and staying in bed in the company of a big ice cream tub? Its despair, and it's a feeling that pops about when we don't get the outcomes that we expect. Despair offers us a reason to give up on our ultimate objectives. In reality, despair may be a good encouragement to take a little break and relax before trying to achieve a tough objective.

4.2 What are the Origins of Unpleasant Feelings, and why are we Getting them?

If you start a bit further questioning unpleasant feelings, you will actually start to understand what could trigger or activate them, and the reason we have them in the very first instance.

In terms of triggers, for example, there may be a variety of things:

Feeling anxiety regarding taking a new job interview

Rage at being stuck up in traffic

Sadness about witnessing a break-up

Annoyance that the preparation for a major project has not been completed by a friend

Despair by not being able to adhere to a new routine by exercise

Emotions are a stream of knowledge that lets you grasp what's all around you. In fact, pessimistic feelings will help you recognize risks and feel able to cope with possible hazards in a constructive way.

Many distinct events throughout our lives, to varying degrees of severity, can incite multiple emotional responses. As a human being, in reaction to constantly evolving circumstances, you will feel a wide repertoire of emotions during your lifespan.

For several people, this is a typical problem: how can we cope with unpleasant feelings that keep showing up while we are exhausted or hurt? Can we put aside our rage and resentment and believe there is no such thing as this, so we can reduce the impact of such emotions? Or do we risk making it worse by doing it wrong? As it works out, "stuffing feelings" is certainly not the best option, and everybody should use simple techniques.

However, if you've asked what to do with these thoughts, you're not alone in dealing with detrimental feelings. Several individuals have the same concern about distress and coping. If they feel overwhelmed by negative emotions such as damage, annoyance or rage, they realize they shouldn't say they feel nothing, yet they don't want to focus on negative emotions and fixate either. But since the majority of us have known that these are not safe stress management techniques, what alternate options do we have?

Dealing with Unpleasant Feelings

Ignoring emotions is not a healthy way to cope with them (like "tucking your anger"). Broadly speaking, it doesn't render them go away but will allow them to pop out in various ways. This is because the feelings function assigns to you about something you're doing wrong in life.

It may be a sign to feel irritated or upset that something has to improve. You will appear to be affected by them if you do not adjust the circumstances or thinking processes that create these unpleasant feelings.

They will even create issues with your physical and mental wellbeing when you are not coping with the concerns you have.

However, rumination, or even the propensity to focus on frustration, dissatisfaction and other negative thoughts, often has health effects. So listening to the emotions is crucial and then taking action to get them out.

Grasp your feelings

Look inward to attempt to find the circumstances of your life that cause tension and unpleasant feelings.

Unpleasant feelings may emerge from a triggering event: for instance, an excessive workload.

Negative feelings are often the outcome of our emotions regarding an occurrence; how we perceive what occurred will affect how we view the incident and whether it creates discomfort or not.

The key task of your feelings is to get you to understand the problem so that you can make the required changes.

Adjust If You May

From my first advice, take what you've absorbed and brought it into effect. Cut down on the triggers of stress, and less likely, you will catch yourself experiencing unpleasant feelings.

This may involve:

Cutting down on stress at work.

Trying to learn assertive communication methods (so you don't feel crushed by individuals).

Change harmful ways of perception via a mechanism known as cognitive rehabilitation.

Seek an Outlet

Making improvements in your life will alleviate unpleasant feelings, but your tension factors may not be totally removed. You may still need to find safe outlets to cope with these feelings when you create improvements in your life to reduce anger.

Daily workout may offer both a cognitive boost and a harmful emotions outlet.

Meditation will help you find some internal "space" in which to function, so your feelings don't feel that stressful.

Seeking ways to have fun with your life and have some happiness will also shift your outlook and alleviate tension.

Find any of these sources, even as unpleasant feelings emerge, you'll be less stressed.

For constant tension relief, you may also want to follow healthier alternatives. Offer them an opportunity, and you'll be less anxious.

Chapter 5: Jealousy

Jealousy is among the most normal and disturbing of all the feelings

humans display. Even if many of us know better, it appears to pull out the worst of us. It's an age-old question, reported since biblical times, and probably encountered much before that. And it's still not exclusive to people. And wild mammals such as chimpanzees and elephants demonstrate jealous behavior.

5.1 What is Jealousy?

It is a normal misjudgment that jealousy is a symbol of affection.

Last week I saw the following quotation on Twitter, from a person whose profile at least indicated that the person was affiliated with psychology: "People that are truly in love are jealous of dumb stuff." I was shocked to find this myth so profoundly rooted that even emotionally educated people believe it.

Envy may be a big partnership concern — a poll undertaken by relational therapists revealed that relational envy was a significant issue for a third of their clients. I intend to dissipate the misconception that jealousy is a love symbol. But if this isn't the case, then what actually motivates jealous acts? Analysis has linked many characteristics to greater jealousy:

1. Having low self-esteem

2. Neuroticism: a common propensity to be mentally unstable, nervous, and moody.

3. Feelings of confusion.

4. Dependence on your partner: Also, telling the audience to assume they don't have successful alternate spouses contributes to more negative responses to imaginary situations that cause jealousy.

5. Thoughts of inferiority in your relationship: concern that you are not nice enough for your spouse in general.

6. An insecure attachment style: A persistent orientation towards intimate partnerships that includes anxiety that your spouse will abandon you or not value you enough. Research has found that momentarily allowing people to feel more firmly connected, by encouraging them to worry about getting help from a loved one, helps them respond less intensely to a hypothetical jealousy persuading situation.

Both of these jealousy causes are for the emotions of insecure individuals, not about the affection they have for their mate.

And what can you do when your mate shows unjustified jealousy?

You need to know that the jealousy of your companion is not really about you; it is all about them. React to Jealous Expressions by comforting your love partner. Evidence has shown that many of those who react to the jealousy of spouses by convincing them of their commitment and affection appear to have relationships that are more secure.

Jealousy styles

Jealousy can better be split down into two big categories: usual and extreme. As already stated, at some stage, everyone feels insecure, no matter how holy they might be. Dr. Hupka states that any form of circumstance that triggers jealousy may be linked to labels. Some of them comprise:

Romantic jealousy: Dr. Hupka and several others agree that the most often encountered form of natural jealousy is potentially romantic envy. Indeed, as per PBS Nightly Business Correspondent, the first battle between romantic couples typically includes jealousy, while couples generally later move on to arguing over financial issues. Amusingly, a 2004 analysis conducted in Evolutionary Psychology indicates that participants of both sexes showed more jealousy over their partner's emotional infidelity when asked over physical vs. emotional infidelity.

Work or Influence Jealousy: this process literally hits people jealous of a "missed" advancement, compensation amount or other work-related problem.

Friend jealousy: Individuals are always afraid of "losing" a buddy to an opportunist.

Family jealousy: One hallmark trait of this form of resentment is sibling rivalry.

Extreme jealousy: Extreme jealousy, like tragic, insane, pathological, paranoid or nervous jealousy, is sometimes characterized by either a variety of adjectives. As per Dr. Hupka, abnormal jealousy may be related to typical problems like intense depression, immaturity and becoming a "control freak." Although, in certain situations, it is due to a mental disorder, such as anxiety or schizophrenia, or a chemical disturbance throughout the brain.

Paranoia and schizophrenia may give birth to illusions of dishonesty and induce a jealous attitude. The strong vulnerability can also lead to jealousy in situations when an entity perceives a danger to the partnership where there is no harm. When it transforms into neurotic envy, it is not possible to know.

"The latter is typically synonymous with maintaining undue influence over the mate, who has irrational worries regarding the mate's loyalty. Sufferers of this type of extreme envy also display habits such as constantly calling the mate to "verify" and scrolling through the mate's mobile and email.

What are you going to do when you are jealous?

When you're the one prying into your partner's inbox, how do you cope with jealousy? Many acts will assist you to cope:

1. Avoid scenarios that are likely to elicit false assumptions. Findings showed in one sample that people who felt jealous appeared to track the Facebook operation of their spouses. The more they spied on Facebook, the more facts they will discover to complain about,

contributing to yet more surveillance and a revolving spiral of heightened control and jealousy.

2. Work with yourself. Act to develop your faith in yourself and in your partnership.

3. Talk with Your companion. If you're feeling envy, speak to your partner about it — but the way you're communicating about it is key: if you're showing rage or sarcasm or hurling your spouse's allegations, it won't improve. You have to be clear forward but not aggressive. Explain the concerns respectfully and explore ways to pursue a remedy. This would help you to feel more satisfied and stop confounding your partner with your jealous behavior. These coping techniques are more likely to yield constructive reactions to your partner.

Jealousy is often justified: For example, if your wife has had an abortion and has violated your confidence, it is a major concern. If you are jealous because you are engaged with someone who may not want monogamy, though you do, therefore, your insecure feelings might be a valid excuse to exit the partnership and search for someone whose partnership priorities are more aligned with yours. But when you get jealous of "stupid stuff," you do not display love; you expose insecurities of your own.

5.2 Why People Feel Jealous?
Insecurity

By far, insecurity is the most prevalent cause of jealousy. People also throw around the phrase "inferiority complex," which isn't a psychological term, but relates to an intrinsic poor ego or low self-esteem — a jealous guy who feels inadequate in his intimate relationships, for example, doesn't feel sure that he's nice and desirable enough to hold another individual involved in him. It's important to remember that in men and women, vulnerability is typically not absolute. In other terms, a woman can be brilliant and highly successful at work as a high-powered lawyer while her psychopathology (becoming jealous) comes out throughout her intimate relationships. Is she, basically, an insecure person? No, however, in her intimate affairs, she has the potential to become intensely insecure.

Obsessive thinking

In virtually any friendship she has, the latest female client of mine in her late 20s, whom I will name Tania, finds herself feeling insecure. She also satisfies certain guidelines for obsessive-compulsive disorder psychologically, even if she may not follow the maximum definition requirements. The brain of Tania appears to run on endless shifts, creating fresh anxieties and fears at all times. Since this is her general style of thought, anyone of her romantic partnerships ultimately seeps into her ability to overanalyze and obsess over stuff. The toughest thing on the planet to handle for obsessed personalities is confusion, including The Unpredictable. While most individuals can withstand a reasonable amount of confusion, she cannot accept the unexpected when Tania's boyfriend reaches home late (why is he late, what was he up to). Her subconscious fills in the blanks as she is confused about where her lover was and created reactions, all of which are derogatory. Quite sometimes, she ends up with evidence produced out of pure nothingness regarding the possible infidelity of her partner and therefore becomes intensely nervous and jealous. If she had no obsessive thinking style, she would have been much less jealous.

Paranoid Personality

Many individuals with whom I have interacted get jealous, but in fact, their jealousy comes from a generally paranoid attitude to certain things in existence. Although paranoia takes the shape of the Schizophrenia-Paranoid Category at the most extreme end of the continuum, the overwhelming majority of paranoid people fell to the relatively mild end of this spectra. Both men and women have certain paranoid features, but their anxiety is not serious enough to reach the definition of paranoid illness in full-blown fashion. Individuals with slight to moderate anxiety find it very difficult to believe people and sometimes suspect sinister intent on the intentions of others. Sometimes they have a sort of attitude that drives them to feel victimized and humiliated, sometimes believing that individuals are out to get them. Sometimes they believe that individuals are attempting to undermine them, their ambitions or their jobs. They, too, sometimes perceive that people, even though observers advise them differently, have set them down, dismissed them, or patronized them. Lastly, Individuals with a paranoid type of behavior are frequently blamers, pointing fault on others as opposed to turning inward and taking liability for their own shortcomings or failures. Too many, they get insecure and grasp a firm conviction that their spouse is cheating, and they will not be reassured differently by any amount of proof.

Reality

If you ask a jealous person if he or she was right to feel jealous, he will usually mention a few instances when, in reality, jealousy was established. In other terms, the companion was really lying, or was really betraying him! The query becomes: Is there a jealousy trend, or is this a unique incident? An individual may be called a jealous individual correctly if she (or he) has a record of being jealous with several partners, several or maybe all of whom did nothing to warrant it. When you're in a relationship with someone that allows you to develop strong feelings of jealousy, question yourself if you've been jealous of other lovers in the past, or whether these thoughts are purely attributable to your new partnership.

If you don't have a past of being insecure, the chances are that your jealous emotions are simply not a concern with your present partnership. In reality, your intuition may indicate you are in a partnership with someone you might not be willing to trust. You're not "the insecure kind" in this scenario; you're more worried and distrustful. Getting a person marking you as insecure when you don't have a past of jealousy is a symbol of mislabeling your emotions. You're not jealous of such a scenario; you're justifiably concerned.

5.3 Pathological Jealousy and Healthy Jealousy

Jealousy is a complex and popular emotion expressed by humans that ranges through relationships and societies, in types and multitudes. It is described as "feeling anger towards others because of the competition, achievement, or benefits of that entity." The description suggests that a rival's impression is necessary for the emotion to appear; without taking into account whether the rival really exists. In communities, in the workplace, in partnerships, and in intimate relationships, it is a sensation that can increase. Evolutionary psychologists' most popular understanding of this sensation derives from "The Basic Inherent Module Concept." Jealousy is an intrinsic feeling, according to this hypothesis, which is driven by a limited collection of neurons in reaction to perceived dangers in the form of sexual partnerships. The theory implies, on the one side, that jealousy in men is an unconscious predisposition geared towards the physical infidelity of their spouse, and, but on the other hand, the theory indicates that the sensation of jealousy in women is inherently predisposed to the mental infidelity of their spouse. The sensation of jealousy is also mistaken with envy, which is described as "a painful or resentful knowledge of another's benefit, coupled with a desire to have the same value." Envy varies from jealousy by means that the former emotion is encountered when an individual desires something that another person has, whilst the latter is an extreme emotion conveyed when a person worries that someone or something may be taken away from the person him/herself. However, under some conditions, envy, especially in intimate relationships, may become unreasonable and harmful. Psychopathic jealousy, often identified as morbid jealousy, psychotic jealousy, or Othello's Syndrome, is an uncommon type of jealousy that frequently expresses itself as an OCD and occurs in interpersonal relationships. Morbidly jealous persons create a definitive proof of disloyalty through meaningless scenarios. Under this sort of resentment, one of the partners is of the opinion that he or she has exclusive control of another person; and that this possession is a requirement to sustain the bond. While the word "Othello's syndrome" implies the condition is irreducible, pathological envy can be regarded as a generic term for the consequence of a variety of different medical conditions. This feeling derives from deep insecurities, unwanted emotions, and a nervous state of wanting to be in charge and feel comfortable. The presence of this condition can be related to multiple factors like addiction to liquor and non-alcoholic drugs, organic brain abnormalities, neurosis, personality disorders, schizophrenia or any psychiatric illness, such as depression, that is marked by irregular mood disorders.

Some pathological jealousy signs include:

• Allegations of staring at other citizens or showing attention to them.

• Criticizing the partner's actions.

• Interrogation of mobile calls and all other contact processes.

• To go through the assets of the spouse.

• Constant checking about the location and the partner's company.

• Isolation of the partner

• Reciprocating the spouse in search of private desires.

• Laying requirements with respect to interaction with the social group of the spouse.

• Accusations of having relationships as a consequence of violence, as sexual activity reduces.

• Suffering from inadequate validation.

• Loss of faith.

• Verbal and/or physical abuse towards the spouse, the person perceived to be the competitor or both.

• Accusing the companion and providing a pretext for jealous behavior.

• Refusing the actions of jealousy, unless cornered.

Overvaluing a concept is described as' a reasonable, understandable concept that the patient pursues outside the limits of rationality. The notion is not opposed, and while it is not a misconception, the patient assigns considerable value to examining and preserving the integrity of the spouse at a significant personal loss even to the partner's pain. Oversold ideas are defined as being ego-syntonic in the person's own thoughts; implying that the opinions project attitudes, beliefs, and emotions that are associated with the person's ego's wishes and objectives, or compatible with the individual's desired self-image, the ideas are often rational but not opposed.

A pathologically jealous person lays forth doubts about their partner's infidelity. The entity then transforms to become possessed as soon as the suspicions are created, and signs of the condition begin to appear. The accused "significant other" is deemed guilty in possession of the grisly jealous spouse, before proof of innocence is discovered. However, the truth does not materialize, and valiant attempts to prove remorse or refute blame fail when unfounded fears are not rationally debunked in the suspect partner's head. In addition, an accusation of infidelity by the accused spouse may spur anger and abuse. In such situations, the forgiving spouse, troubled by constant interrogations and allegations of infidelity, can offer false confessions that create rage in the jealous person.

A comprehensive medical background can be taken into consideration in order to determine psychopathology. An appraisal could include:

The past of psychotic and affective illnesses.

• The past of abuse.

• The reliability of the partnership.

• The past of abuse of drugs.

• The complete past of the person previous to his or her involvement with the present partner.

In order to define the structure of morbid jealousy, to research any associated psychopathology, and to research the probability of the presence of an endogenous condition, psychopathological evaluation should be accompanied by a mental state test. Finally, the risk evaluation of both spouses must be carried out, and the risk of suicide, the record of sexual abuse, the incidence of physical violence, involving some third individual (e.g., alleged competitor), and the risk to children (if any) should be addressed.

5.4 How to Avoid Getting Jealous

Consider insecurities of your own

Our own insecurities reside underneath the emotions of envy, which might seem like problems of self-esteem or the worries you have when contrasting yourself to someone. Fear of rejection is also focused on jealousy. If you feel jealous, then strive to confront the insecurity.

Consider all the qualities that you contribute to the partnership and all the stuff that your partner feels they appreciate about you. Try to note that your partner prefers to be with you. If you still feel jealous of a certain person in your SO's life, consider deleting their Instagram, so you have fewer possibilities to equate yourself to them. Not only are the constant similarities needless, but they'll also only make you sound much worse.

For your partnership, create somewhat reasonable standards

Finding other people appealing from time to time is absolutely

natural. It doesn't have to be a challenge unless the companion is obnoxious with their sexuality or flirting publicly with someone. It is essential to develop reasonable relationship perceptions and recognize that you cannot control the behavior of someone else. "With the intention of empathy and respect towards each other, you should express your thoughts with your spouse, speak freely and frankly, and work for a shared understanding.

Remember where the problems of confidence come from

Jealousy in a partnership will help carry the root problems to the forefront. If you have not completely worked past childhood anxieties or infidelity from a prior relationship, for instance, it may show up in the way you act in your present relationship. Recognize where the emotions come from when you converse with the mate. "Be responsible for your actions and commit to overcoming your feelings or past problems that contribute to envy.

Trying the Strategy of the Rubber Band

Place a rubber band on your wrist, and pop the rubber band every time you start to find yourself falling into jealousy. The rubber band method is a strategy for practitioners that are correlated with understanding how to tolerate uncomfortable feelings or thinking easier. This is generally deemed a method of anxiety tolerance, something that allows you to regroup at the instant. More importantly, after feeling conflicting feelings, people are instructed to "pop" themselves with the rubber band as a cue to relax, take a breather, and examine what's going on.

Talk it over with a therapist or a buddy

Although it is necessary to have a chat with your companion about how you feel, it may be especially useful to speak about your insecurity problems with someone who can offer an objective viewpoint about what's going about. Your friend can be there to hear you while you talk.

Having a competent therapist's guidance will also allow you to move with and conquer the emotions that have you trapped. It requires strength and bravery to dive through fragile, insecure emotions, but it can be empowering and allow for recovery, improvement, and personal development."

Be transparent and frank about your feelings

Lately, if you've been overwhelmed by jealousy, it might be best to have a transparent and frank talk with your spouse regarding how you feel and why you might feel this way. "Tell, talk, talk! "I realize it can sound repetitive, boring and cliché, and it's really that crucial. In many instances, jealousy is an inner struggle, so take action and get to realize and concentrate on yourself. And discuss your conclusions with your spouse. Clarify to them how you think, what makes you insecure and build limits for yourself and your partnership."

Practice Gratitude

Learning respect and acceptance for what you've received can help you concentrate on the positives of the partnership. Reflect on what your mate does for you more than what they don't do, or all the moments that they're there for you and when they aren't. If you cannot see anything good, maybe it's time to move forward.

Remember how jealousy impacts you adversely

It is worth your time to reflect on how adversely your jealousy affects you as a person. Being continually on the verge, for example, when your wife is listening to or messaging others, is not good for you or your marriage. You will be more able to find out how to get beyond jealousy and let it go by completely coming to grips with how jealousy is affecting you or having you behave and act.

Regardless of how you handle your emotions, it's crucial to note that it's not the responsibility of your spouse to comfort you or to "fix" the problems that trigger jealousy. Your emotions are your duty and are for you, not your circumstance or spouse.

Emphasis on the bad or the good

One approach to get over your jealousy feelings is by changing the emphasis. The most liberating thing you might do in a partnership is to let go of fears over what could go bad and concentrate on what's going well. I advise concentrating on the stuff your partner does that you're thankful for and convincing yourself that you're more than enough for your partner every day.

Write it out

A diary is a wonderful way to maintain track of your jealousy-related insecurities and complaints, while it's best for venting. I advise focusing on your partnership and posing concerns such as, is your spouse still the best guy for you? Have they done anything specific to bring about jealousy? "If so, then this is a deal breaker. If not, question yourself if you ought to look into your partnership differently. Do you carry your history into this current relationship? Are you self-sabotaging? It might be time to attempt to save your relationship by trying something better!"

Don't hold onto jealousy

Your safest bet is to continue to let go of the jealousy that is dragging you down unless you're convinced your partner is cheating. Practice self-care strategies to improve self-esteem, such as yoga and trips with mates. When you don't look, the happier you feel for yourself, the more you will let go about what others do." she notes.

Instead of making yourself dwell in jealousy, in your partnership, you may choose to take measures to experience less of the hated feeling. Try some of these strategies the next time you sense jealousy building up, and you may notice that handling the emotions becomes much simpler.

Chapter 6: How to stop neediness in a relationship

Are you concerned that maybe you are too clingy or too needy?

When you are in a partnership, it is easy to cross lines. Especially if you are in love with anyone, even if you think maybe you're too clingy, don't worry. With a few quick tweaks, you can fix the behavior.

6.1 How to Stop Being Clingy

But first, why is it that people get clingy?

Our previous psychiatric and mental traumas profoundly affect how we respond to harmful emotions.

Psychologists have shown that the key factor of how we treat our adult partnerships is something termed "attachment style."

The method we connect with our significant adult spouses bears traces from our early interactions with our kin.

Individuals with a stable environment are capable of "safe commitment." Without becoming clingy, they will respect their partnerships.

On the opposite, you could be insecurely dependent if you grew up in a dysfunctional climate.

This form of association will manifest itself in two ways.

If you're anxiously linked, you're too susceptible to hints your partner's about to leave you. You become excessively reliant on your intimate partners as a consequence.

In comparison, individuals who are strong on avoidance of attachment do not want to create relational ties with their spouses."

If you decide to be with your companion always, you could have an unstable attachment. Being clingy is just the reaction to concerns regarding the separation.

Currently, whether you are firmly connected or insecurely attached does not matter. There are also many avenues to develop a friendship with your spouse that is safe.

Recognize you can have an issue

By realizing why it may be dangerous, you're also beginning to take ownership of becoming clingy.

The very first step is acknowledging the dilemma of being clingy.

It's no embarrassment admitting you're too clingy. And there are typically positive explanations that you are this way, including early childhood anxieties.

Healthy partnerships are worth a fortune, so do something about it if you have a propensity to be too needy. Act to resolve the wounds of the past and build stronger potential partnerships.

Activate His Hero Reflex

I'm mindful of what you think:

Why would it encourage me to avoid being insecure and clingy by treating my guy like a hero?

Treating your guy as a hero when he wants more space sounds odd, but it's actually the most counter-intuitive thing you can do.

Males have a built-in wish to be their wife's provider and guardian.

And if you're too clingy and manipulating his attitude, you don't allow him the space he wants to perform this for you.

He can't take the opportunity to jump for you into the plate because he feels capitulated in. Above all, men ought to behave of their own initiative and according to their impulses.

In psychology, there's currently a recent hypothesis that's causing a lot of excitement at the moment. And that gets to the core of why needy girlfriends and wives ought to offer liberty to their husbands to be their hero.

It's called the intuition of a hero.

A guy has to feel like he's a defender, provider and important to the lady he's searching for. And she loves him for that.

To put it another way, he would feel like some kind of hero. Not a Thor-like action hero, but a champion to her.

I realize it might all sound crazy. Women do not require anyone in this day and age to save them. In their lives, they don't require a 'hero.'

But it loses the argument of what the feeling of a hero is all about.

The hero urge is an instinctive urge in the life of men to stand up to the woman's plate. This is profoundly ingrained in the genetics of males.

A man is required to be one, even if women do not require a hero. And if you want him in your partnership to be satisfied, then you'll have to let him be.

But how do you evoke in him this impulse?

In an authentic manner, the key is to make him sound like a hero. And there are items that you can tell, texts that you can give, suggestions you can create that would not in any way make you come off as clingy or vulnerable.

Know how to live with the anxiety

Concerns of separation, unstable commitment, etc.—all of these are attributed to anxiety.

You're nervous, and any moment you're not with your girlfriend, you fear something terrible will happen.

And how can you deal with that?

Because tension plays such a significant role in the process, finding how to recognize and deal with the circumstances that cause your insecure attachment instincts is the best way to escape the fall into clinginess and misery.

By considering the future of your relationship, instead of dreaming of the worst, I believe in creating a "secure foundation of a bond."

Even you can handle your everyday tension by utilizing "constructive means of coping."

When you feel emotionally disoriented, you are more inclined to drill into your own vulnerability, which renders you more vulnerable to a partner's potential rejection.

By implementing coping mechanisms that both make you feel comfortable, and help you resolve the circumstances that stress you out, improve your resilience.

Work on yourself

This persists all the time:

People are in a partnership, and unexpectedly they ignore their own personal progress and development.

Acting clingy is a symptom of the loss of self-love.

Losing yourself in a partnership may trigger fear, anger, or even despair, and can lead you to revolt or express yourself in unrealistic or drastic ways that may endanger the bond.

Work for yourself, too.

Incite the companion to do the same too.

This would enable you to be happier individuals. But it's just going to make you a better couple as well.

When each individual is able to see improvement as an incentive for development and the potential for an autonomous self within the partnership, it would, in turn, foster a healthy relational atmosphere.

(You need to always assert control over your own influence if you want to avoid being clingy and in need.

Develop your self-esteem

One of the biggest factors, why we stay clingy to our spouses is that we're scared to sacrifice them.

This is perfectly natural. Particularly in our relationships, we all need stability.

The propensity, however, may manifest itself in severe clinginess.

Researchers also have shown in a 2013 analysis that self-esteem significantly affects the happiness of your connection with your partner.

To develop your self-confidence if you'd rather be less clingy but more happily confident in your partnership.

Be physically and emotionally accountable for yourself. Establish your own profession. Do what gives you purpose. All of these will help create trust.

"Trust is sexy," as they claim. And undoubtedly, your partner would believe the same thing.

Establish confidence in your partnership

We're going to face it:

You have difficulties with confidence. Else, you wouldn't be so needy.

It's difficult to trust your partner, particularly when you're full of nervous thoughts about "what if."

But if you have no basis to doubt your spouse, then why is the fear running through your mind?

Couples who do not trust will not feel safe because their partnership can cycle through repeated peaks and lows of emotion.

"This is because a mistrustful spouse invests a majority of their time scrutinizing their partnership and seeking to recognize the

intentions of their spouse."

Sounds like you?

So it's time to build your partner's faith.

Free yourself from all the pessimistic feelings. If anything terrible happens, it's going to happen.

Strive to provide more room for your partner.

Going against your normal state of clinginess is difficult so strive to offer more room to your mate.

Couples ought to leave each other space. Dating intensely doesn't involve every minute needing to be together. Time together is undoubtedly one indication of how good love is. It's always risky to bring so much money together in time as the wellbeing partnership predictor.

So allow space for your companion to breathe.

If you're in a long-distance partnership, following the tip is highly important.

Let him feel necessary (without being needy)

Let him feel necessary without getting bogged down

Men have a passion built-in for something that extends above sexual intimacy.

Men plainly put, in his life, have a biological desire to feel important to the woman. What always divides "joy" from "lust"

is seeming important.

This biological urge drives men to care for women and to defend them. He needs to stand up for her, feel significant, and be respected for his efforts.

Without becoming either clingy or vulnerable, how do you make him sound vital?

In an adequate way, the trick is to make him feel special.

The stuff that you will say, the messages that you can submit and the suggestions you can create to activate his hero instinct automatically make the difference.

Mostly I don't give any attention to common modern psychological ideas. I believe, however, the hero impulse is a convincing example of what fuels men romantically.

No one tells women to need a savior to take better care of them. Women will change a tire today, open their own pots, and care for themselves in life overall.

That still doesn't mean that men always don't want to appear like one, while women do not require a hero.

That's why it's crucial for women to learn more about the hero impulse and how they can leverage it to their advantage.

Chapter 7: Self-Evaluation of Anxiety in a Relationship

We also recognize that an essential aspect of achievement may be self-esteem. Little or no self-esteem may leave a sense of loss or despair

in people. It may even cause people to make poor decisions, collapse into relationships of failure or struggle to measure up to their maximum potential.

On the other side, an extravagant idea of self-importance may be off-putting to some and can also hurt relationships. It may also be a symptom of a narcissistic personality, a mental condition defined by a desire for undue admiration and a loss of empathy towards other people.

7.1 Self Esteem – Understanding and Fixing Low Self Esteem

Self-esteem levels may be dangerous at the severe extreme ends of the continuum, so typically it is essential to obtain an equilibrium right in the center. Generally, a practical and optimistic image of oneself is known to be the norm. So what is self-esteem precisely? Where does it originate from, and what is its true effect on our lives?

What is Self-Esteem?

The word self-esteem is used in psychology to define the general sense of self-worth or important sense of an entity. To put it another way, how much you like and admire yourself. It requires a set of opinions about oneself, such as evaluating your own body, beliefs, thoughts, and habits.

Self-esteem is also seen as a characteristic of personality, implying it appears to be healthy and lasting.

Why Self-esteem Is Necessary

Self-esteem can have a crucial role in your life drive and achievement. Low self-esteem can keep you from thriving at work or school since you don't consider yourself to be good.

By comparison, you can develop high self-esteem by managing life with an optimistic, assertive outlook and trusting that you will accomplish your objectives.

Self-Esteem Theories

A lot of theorists have written about the complexities of self-esteem. In the system of criteria of psychologist Abraham Maslow, the desire for self-esteem plays an essential part, which describes self-esteem as one of the central human motives.

Maslow indicated that persons require both recognition from other persons and inner self-respect. In essence, for an entity to evolve as a person and attain self-actualization, all of these requirements must be met.

It is necessary to remember that self-esteem is a term different from self-efficacy, which includes how good you think your potential behavior, results, or skills can be managed.

7.2 Factors Influencing Self-Esteem

Many variables affect self-esteem, as you may expect. The self-esteem will be affected by your inner thought, age, any possible disorders, illnesses, or physical deficiencies, and your work.

In addition, hereditary influences that help define the personality of an individual may play a part, but mostly it is our interactions that form the foundation for the overall self-esteem. For instance, those who regularly obtain highly supportive or derogatory evaluations from family and peers will possibly encounter low self-esteem.

Balanced Self-Esteem Indicators

There are a few easy ways to know whether you're feeling safe for yourself. If you are more inclined to: You possibly have high self-esteem.

Stop focusing on recent, detrimental interactions.

Expressing the desires

• Feel motivated

• Take an optimistic view on life

Tell "no" when you intend to

• See and consider common strengths and limitations.

• Indications of poor Self-Esteem

If you happen to have these typical issues triggered by low self-esteem, you may need to focus on how you view yourself:

• You presume people are better than you.

• You find it hard to communicate your wishes

• You concentrate on the flaws

• Emotions such as guilt, sadness, or anxiety are also encountered.

• You have a pessimistic approach to life

• You have a severe fear of defeat.

• You have problems embracing the supportive reviews

• You have difficulty saying 'no.'

• You place the interests of other persons above your own.

Using CBT to develop self-esteem

The key objectives of the CBT plan are to recognize and crack

the unhelpful cycles that hold low self-esteem running and to generate more healthy and practical perceptions. This includes understanding and addressing harmful prejudices, unhelpful principles and attitudes which are self-defeating.

Record of Activity:

It is also challenging for individuals with poor self-esteem, especially when combined with depression and low mood, to engage in pleasurable and rewarding activities. This is because they are not inspired, or they may be unworthy of pleasure, or because they have busy work hours. For starters, Sarah spends all her time supporting others; Hannah works so intensely that she has practically no time for relaxing and enjoyment, and Kevin neglects his fitness and health because he thinks he is not worth caring for. Individuals with poor self-esteem will neglect themselves. It will strengthen poor self-esteem and render you more likely to depression and stress if you do not look after yourself. The purpose of monitoring your behavior is to help you take better care of yourself, make your life happier, offer yourself recognition for your everyday successes, and find the right balance between work, leisure, and relaxing.

Stage 1: Maintaining a diary of events

Now, look at how you invest your time and ask how rewarding you find your schedule and everyday tasks. For a week, it will help you do something systematically by documenting what you are doing on a report sheet – breaking the day into pieces. As soon as you can, it is important to document each behavior, since leaving it for longer than a few hours can find it harder to recall how you thought and negative thoughts will affect how you recall it. The principle is to document everyday experiences along with ratings on how rewarding each activity feels. Activities may be rewarding as they are pleasurable or giving you a feeling of accomplishment. Using the letter P and a 0-10 figure to denote how pleasurable an exercise was, with 'P0' meaning an event was not pleasurable at all, and 'P10' suggesting an activity was highly pleasurable. Use the letter A and a number from 0 to 10 to evaluate how much accomplishment from action was felt.

Examples include:

3-4 pm: children retrieved from school & store visited: P1, A65-2pm: consumers served at a job: P6, A66

It is important to take into consideration how you think at the moment for the accomplishment score because you award yourself praise for how much work you place into the operation. For starters, when feeling good and looking forward to the day in front, it might be easier to get out of bed, but it may be a challenge when feeling unwell on a tough day, and may thus merit a higher achievement ranking. Here is an illustration of how Kevin has not given sufficient credit to himself:

For months, he held off going to the bank and felt guilty of the financial problems, thinking the bank's employees would be dismissive and disapproving. When he actually persuaded himself to go to the bank, he earned himself an accomplishment ranking of only 3. "His rationale was" this should be simple, most individuals go to the bank without worrying about it. His success ranking, therefore, neglected to take into consideration his unique cases and the emotional work needed to tackle everything he dreaded. Not allowing ourselves credit for the work we put into stuff will decrease enthusiasm and hold low self-esteem and depression running.

Stage 2: What do you intend to change?

When you've held the journal for about a week, it's time to worry about how you're managing your time and ask what you'd like to alter.

Consider the issues below:

What was, and what was not enjoyable? What improvements will you create to create your everyday life and tasks more rewarding?

Do you look after yourself and handle yourself as though you're a deserving person? When you supported somebody you cared for and tried to handle yourself right, what improvements will you be making?

Do you find a balance between, on the one hand, fun hobbies, leisure and stuff for yourself and, on the other, jobs, assignments, items for other people? What can you do to build a healthier balance, if not?

Will you recognize your everyday successes in the way that anyone else might? Low self-esteem and anxiety sometimes cause individuals to discount their successes. If this is an issue for you, then it might be beneficial to practice by remembering accomplishments. Try to take note of how you feel at the moment and how much work the task took.

Is inactivity a concern for you? Depression and fear frequently cause persons to become idle and to stop operations. This indicates they are looking for fun and a feeling of accomplishment. One of the most important methods of raising energy levels and attitude is to schedule a steady improvement in your everyday activities.

Have pessimistic feelings get in the way of achieving stuff? If they did, write them down and attempt to challenge them, as later mentioned.

Stage 3: Make adjustments and task preparation.

When you have thoughts on the sort of improvements you'd like to make, the next step would require realistic checking of this out. This can be achieved by thinking forward to the week, arranging realistic tasks for each day, and preparing for a more fulfilling schedule. Try to find a compromise with jobs, exercise and leisure, if you may – the things that have to be performed and those you wish to avoid. Then consider something more achievable if this is too excessive when even a little change a day will make a difference. Study their effect after you have attempted to make improvements. If the modifications relate to an improvement in your happiness and performance, then you will expand on them. You will figure out what went wrong if the improvements turn out to be unhelpful, and take this detail into consideration as you make future adjustments.

Richards discovered that being involved brought him a better sense of having charge of his life and finding it important to do anything. Small measures helped him develop wounded confidence. He then witnessed a chain response phenomenon that he was encouraged to try to do something more.

Track positive signs:

Earlier, it identified the negative prejudices that play a role in retaining low self-esteem. You can notice how Sarah takes all derogatory remarks she gets to heart, and she denies or discounts moments when people are nice to her or give her compliments. Ignoring your positive qualities just holds you down in self-esteem, so it prevents you from getting a holistic perspective that takes into consideration your strong attributes as well as the real flaws and stuff you might like to improve. Holding a 'strong record' makes you pay attention to your successful points and successes and lets you adjust your pessimistic core views and perceptions towards yourself favorably, so you can build a more reasonable and rational image towards yourself.

Stage 1: Identify Good attributes

People with poor self-esteem are not necessarily in the practice of spotting their own good traits and abilities, and can sometimes find this challenging. The questions below will help you become more conscious of your good attributes. Look for some pessimistic feelings, such as "that's not special" or "I should have done it differently," that cause you to underestimate your good attributes. Examples of the detrimental biases at work are these. Learn not to let them hinder your good attributes from being noted.

What do you really like regarding yourself, however trivial it can seem?

What, though humble, are the positive attainments of your existence so far? Have you kept any connections, held down a career, become a parent or caretaker or established some expertise relevant to your career, home life, social habits and interests? Do you know how to drive, swim, cook, knit, use a machine, and do housework, planting or DIY, for instance? If you have any expertise in academia, media, athletics, or people?

Which challenges did you strive to overcome? Offer yourself praise for the sacrifices you have created to resolve challenges and anxieties, as this takes bravery and commitment. What will your attributes and talents mean about someone who loves you? You may attempt to ask anyone for advice with this, but be cautious not to ask someone (for instance, a critical mother or spouse) who may have attributed to the low self-esteem.

What characteristics do you like in people that you wish to attain?

What bad traits (being mean or violent, for instance) do you NOT possess? Although you can think of some who don't have this means you have to have positive characteristics (such as being compassionate or respectful).

An illustration of Kevin's collection of values, talents and accomplishments is here:

I didn't have a pleasant time as a kid because my parents were not cooperative, and I didn't get any love or help from them. As a teen, my frustration made it hard for me to fit in a classroom. I felt like I was giving up at the school, but during my last year, I worked hard and managed to finish several evaluations, and I did better than most people had expected. I've got determination.

I did OK at work and was rewarded. Often my coworkers ask for my guidance, and I have got positive feedback from my former career. I am professional at work and informative.

I have several colleagues, a handful of whom I've known for decades. When I was a kid, an instructor really seemed to enjoy me. I am loveable.

I've learned how to use a machine, how to bake, how to drive, how to swim and how to play tennis.

I am normally punctual.

Yeah, I take care of my dog well. I am a caring person.

Have a look at mentioning your good attributes now. You will relate to it when different stuff happens to you. To keep this active, check out the list and recall the moments when you have displayed these characteristics in the past as clearly as you can, and write down these reasons. The next move is to search for confirmation of these values on a regular basis within a few days when you have gone as far as you can with the chart. For a long period of time, you might have been dismissing and undervaluing your good attributes, but regular repetition can make you become more natural when noticing them.

Stage 2: Noting good qualities every day

On a regular basis, write down all proof of your good characteristics and talents. Try capturing about three a day, if you can. Initially, this will be challenging, but with experience, this can become simpler. (This will help you recognize your everyday accomplishments if you have an exercise diary). The aim is to keep this running until you are in the habit of always, without too much effort, recognizing your good attributes. If the issue of poor self-esteem is especially serious, it can take a few months before this becomes more normal or longer.

Note that the record not only mentions features but provides a bit of detail. If you do so, you will read back through your log and recall what's defined in it. It is essential to remember that the explanations should not be earth-shaking and that there are little aspects that matter. Be sure to overlook or dismiss items when you believe they are "insignificant" or "not special" or that you have already recorded something identical. Notice how your happiness improves as your abilities are remembered. The goal is to become so comfortable with your positive points that you can remember them immediately so that your emphasis on your poor points would inevitably be overridden. Check your chart when you're comfortable before heading to bed to strengthen your confidence and awareness of your successes, or put it anywhere you can easily return to it when it hits low mood.

Thought Record:

Low levels of self-esteem can cause people to expect distress and become hyper self-critical. Instead of thinking they are 100 percent real, thought archives would help you challenge and verify these pessimistic thoughts. This will help break down the unhelpful habits of thought and behavior, which generates poor self-esteem.

Stage 1: Capturing bad thoughts and ideas:

The principle is to watch out for occasions that you feel particularly upset. Writing down any distressing incident cannot be realistic or beneficial. You will want to dwell on the hardest few moments or any standard incidents, such that every day you cannot put down more than three instances.

Note down what you did when you were getting angry in the 'scenario' section.

Write down the key feelings you have encountered in the 'emotion' section. (Emotions are typically single terms that are nervous, unhappy, upset, furious, humiliated, ashamed, or irritated, but translating them into terms may be complicated.

Try to capture what was running on in your mind as you were upset and note down this in the 'bad feelings' section. What about the circumstance that disturbed you? Has it caused any self-critical or nervous thinking, or distressing photos or memories?

When you get into the habit of collecting negative thoughts and emotions, maybe after a week of practice, the next move is to challenge certain thoughts and get a healthy and rational viewpoint, as mentioned below.

Stage 2: Pessimistic thought questioning:

The below questions will help you examine your pessimistic feelings to achieve a more balanced mindset.

What is the proof that confirms the thought? What is the proof against it?

What are the alternate views? If they were in your position and had felt like this, what would you suggest to a mate? What could a friend say to you?

Are you forecasting the future? If yes, what might happen to be the worst? What should be done regarding it? What are your professional strengths, how did you deal in the past, what aid, guidance and support are available?

What is the best result which might happen? You will understand how impossible the worst result sounds by exaggerating the best possible outcome.

If there are any biased? Are you leaping to conclusions? Are you speaking in terms of everything or nothing, or demanding yourself to be perfect? Are you dwelling on your flaws and ignoring your strengths?

As emotions are connected to how we mentally feel, remember how you can become less nervous and/or frustrated while questioning a negative idea when thinking becomes more positive and rational.

Experiments on behavior:

Behavioral studies carry the mind log forward when evaluating harmful emotions in reality. You should maintain a record of behavioral tests.

In the first column, the first move is to note down your bad thoughts. These thoughts will come from your log of thoughts.

Then think about how you might test your pessimistic feelings and explain in the 'experiment' section the course of action momentarily.

Note down what you expect will happen in the 'prediction' section before conducting the experiment.

Note down whether your hypothesis was accurate, and what really occurred, after you have conducted the experiment.

Finally, equate the forecast of what happens and note down what you discovered in the final entry.

Taking the chance of being around others and entering new environments, becoming outgoing and assertive, welcoming obstacles and rewards, and doing previously ignored items can help create knowledge that supports more reasonable predictions and forms of thinking. This can be achieved progressively by deciding to execute one experiment per day/week or by reacting differently to possibilities such as rewards.

Having a recorded log of behavioral studies will help you decide if your forecasts appear to be rational or are skewed by subconscious prejudices. But, even though your forecasts seem to be overwhelmingly pessimistic, they might still be correct at times. If you receive unfavorable reviews during an experiment, strive not to misinterpret them out of proportion.

Chapter 8: Anxiety and Miscommunication

Often, openly expressing your thoughts and needs is a vital part of dispute resolution. As you already know, saying the wrong thing may

be like pouring gasoline on a fire and escalating a confrontation. The key thing to note is to be straightforward and assertive in expressing what's in your head, without getting offensive or placing the other party on the defensive.

9.1 Communicating Better in Relationship

One successful dispute solving technique is to use 'I feel' phrases to place it in the perspective of how you feel instead of what you think the other party is doing wrong.

Assertive communication may improve the relationships by-tension reduction and by offering mutual help in periods of difficulty.

A respectful yet assertive "no" to unnecessary demands from others will help you to prevent your schedule from being overrun and encourage peace in your life.

An appreciation of assertive conversation will also help you cope more effectively with challenging families, acquaintances and co-workers, reducing drama and tension. In the end, assertive communication helps you to establish the required limits that help you to fulfill your needs in partnerships without angering others and without enabling irritation and frustration to sneak in. This allows you in partnerships to get everything you need whilst helping your loved ones to satisfy their needs as well. Although many individuals associate assertive communication with tension and disagreement, assertiveness genuinely enables individuals to be stronger.

Assertive engagement requires preparation. Many people misinterpret assertiveness for aggressive behavior, but assertiveness is simply the equilibrium between aggressiveness and timidity on the center ground. Aggressiveness contributes to broken partnerships and wounded feelings. Passivity leads to frustration and resentment, and in the end, often also lashing out.

9.2 Improve Mode of Conversation

Learning to communicate assertively helps you to value the wishes and privileges of others, including your own, and to establish relational expectations while making them feel valued at the same time. These measures will help you establish a healthier style of conversation (and, in the end, alleviate tension in your life).

1. be factual on what you do not want, never be judgmental.

If you ask anyone regarding a pattern you'd like to see improved, adhere to accurate explanations of what they've achieved, instead of utilizing derogatory labels or phrases that express opinions. Take, for instance:

Scenario: Your mate, who typically runs late, turned up for lunch 20 mins late.

Inappropriate answer (aggressive): "You are too disrespectful! You are so late."

Assertive style: "We had to get together at 10:30, but now its 10:50."

Don't presume that you understand what the motivations of the other party are, particularly if you believe they're negative. Do not believe in this case that your friend came intentionally late as they decided not to come or that they appreciate their own time better than yours.

2. Be spot on regarding the behavior's consequences. Don't evaluate or overstretch.

It is an essential start to be realistic about what you do not

appreciate about someone's actions, without overblowing or judging. The same refers to explaining the consequences of their actions. Do not overstate, mark or judge; define only:

"Inappropriate reaction:" Lunch's ruined now.

Assertive style: "Now I have less time for lunch to spend as by 12:00 am, I do need to get back to work."

An assertive style, tone of voice and body language matters. Let your confidence be expressed: stand upright, hold eye contact, and relax. Using a sound that is strong yet welcoming.

3. Using "I messages."

It comes across like criticism or an insult when you start a sentence with "You ..." and puts individuals on guard. If you begin with "I," the emphasis is more on how you experience and how their actions influence you. It also indicates more ownership in the emotions and less liability. This helps reduce other individual's defensiveness, model the act of accepting accountability, and drive both of you towards substantive change. For instance:

Your statement: "You ought to avoid this!" I statement: "I would like you to stop this."

Do not hesitate to respond and pose questions while you're in a debate! Understanding the point of view of the other party is critical.

4. Bringing all together.

Here is a perfect expression that brings it all together: "I sense [your feelings] when you [their conduct]."

This method offers a straightforward, non-attacking, rather responsible means of informing people how their actions affect you when using for objective facts, rather than assumptions or marks. For instance: "I feel assaulted when you scream."

5. List the acts, consequences, and emotions.

"The consequences of their actions are a more advanced version of this model (again, translated into concrete terms), and appears like this:" If you [their conduct], then [their action's results], then I feel [the way you feel].

"For instance:" I have to wait when you come late, and I feel irritated.

Or, "When you advise the children that they may do anything I've already banned, some of my parental power is stripped away, and I feel threatened."

Try to consider win-win: Consider if you can find a solution or a way to fulfill the expectations with all of you. Maybe a new meeting spot will enable them to stay on schedule in the situation of the always-late mate. Or you could just only opt to make reservations at periods when your life is more flexible, and you won't be too overwhelmed by their lateness.

Seek a Plan

When you accept the other person's viewpoint, and they accept yours, it's time to find a compromise to the conflict — a plan that all will work with. Often an easy and logical response pops up if both sides recognize the other individual's perspective. In situations where the dispute was centered on a misconception or a lack of perspective into the viewpoint of the other, a clear clarification will work well, and an accessible conversation will get us together.

On some occasions, it takes a bit more effort. In situations where there is a disagreement about a topic, and both parties don't approve, you have a few options: occasionally you may agree to differ, sometimes you may negotiate a consensus or middle ground, and in some instances, the individual who feels more intensely about a problem can negotiate their path, knowing that they can grant the next time. The main thing is to come to the point of agreement to attempt to sort out problems in a manner that honors everybody concerned.

Notice When It Does Not Work

Because of the burden of a person's unresolved dispute, it is often best to bring any space into the partnership or break links altogether.

Simple dispute mediation strategies will only carry you too far in situations of violence, and personal protection has to take precedence.

On the other hand, when coping with troublesome family members, introducing a few limits and respecting the weaknesses of the other party in the partnership may offer some stability. Letting go can be a tremendous source of tension relief in partnerships that are unsupportive or marked by continuing conflict.5 only you may know whether a partnership should be strengthened or can be let go.

How to strengthen your relations with effective skills in conversation

Conflict is practically unavoidable inside a partnership. Conflict is not a question in itself; nevertheless, the manner it is treated will pull people together or break them apart. Bad communication abilities, conflict and confusion, maybe a cause of frustration and distance or a springboard towards a better friendship and a happy future.

Efficient Communication Tips

Every time you're grappling with confrontation, bear in mind these ideas on good negotiation skills, and you will achieve a more optimistic result. Ok, here's how.

Stay Cantered

Even while coping with current issues, it's easy to dig up past apparently connected disputes. It seems necessary to fix all that concerns you at once to have it all addressed whilst you are still struggling with one disagreement. Unfortunately, this also clouds the dilemma and allows it less possible to achieve common consensus and a remedy to the present problem, thus making the whole debate more challenging and often frustrating.

Try not to dig up wounds or other problems in the past. Keep concentrated on the moment, the thoughts, consider each other and come up with a solution. Mindfulness training on mindfulness will enable you in all aspects of your life to strive to be more aware.

Listen closely

People sometimes believe they are attentive, but while the other individual finishes speaking, they are just worried about what they're going to discuss next. Try to remember it the next time you are in a debate, whether you do so.

Really good communication runs in both directions. Although it may be challenging, strive to genuinely listen to what your partner is telling. But don't disturb it. Do not get protective. Only listen to them and think back on what they mean, because they realize that you've understood it. You will also really appreciate them, and they're more prepared to hear from you.

Try to understand their perspective.

All of us basically want to be noticed and acknowledged in a confrontation. To bring the other individual to see it our way, we speak a tone from our viewpoint. This is reasonable, but too much emphasis will end up backfiring on our own ability to be recognized above all else. Ironically, since we just do this often, there's no emphasis on the viewpoint of the other party, and nobody feels heard.

Try showing the other hand really, and maybe you can describe yours easier. (If you're not 'getting it,' ask further questions before you do.) People would be more inclined to answer if they are listened to.

Answering Critique with Compassion

It's quick to believe they're incorrect and get defensive anytime anyone comes to you with judgment. While feedback is painful to hear and sometimes misunderstood or distorted by the feelings of the other individual, it is necessary to listen to the distress of the other individual and react with respect for their emotions. Look at what is real about what they mean, too; at you, it can be useful knowledge.

Own What's Yours

Understand that personal responsibility is a power, not a shortcoming. Good contact requires knowing that you're mistaken. Suppose all of you bear the blame in a dispute (which is generally the case), search at what is yours and confess to it. This diffuses the case, provides a successful precedent, and reflects maturity. It very also encourages the other individual to react in turn, bringing you all closer to a common understanding and a plan.

Using "I" Messages

It's less confrontational, causes less defensiveness, and lets the other party consider your perspective instead of feeling threatened, instead of doing stuff like, "You really screwed up here," introduce sentences with "I," and making them about yourself and your emotions, such as, "I feel upset when this occurs."

Look for Cooperation

Rather than seeking to "win" the case, search at options that satisfy the needs of both. Either by consensus or a new innovative approach that offers you both what you desire most, this emphasis is far more successful than one party having what they want at the other's cost. A good relationship means seeking a settlement in which all parties will be satisfied.

Taking some time off

Flames get hot at instances, and it's just too hard to pursue a conversation without it being a disagreement or a battle. It's safe to take a break from the conversation before you all cool down if you sense yourself or your spouse beginning to get too upset to be productive or exhibiting any destructive behavioral habits. It may include taking a stroll and cooling back and move to the discussion in an hour, "napping on it" so you can digest what you feel a little better, or anything you feel is the right match for both of you, as long as you return to the discussion. Effective contact sometimes implies understanding when to take a rest.

Keep at It

Although it is often a good idea to take a break from the conversation, it still comes back to it. When each of you handles the issue with a positive mindset, shared interest, and a desire to consider the point of view of the other or at least pursue a compromise, you will make strides in the aim of a dispute resolution. Don't give up talking until it's time to give up on the friendship.

Ask for support if it is important for you.

If either or both of you have difficulty being polite through confrontation, or whether you have attempted to settle tension with your spouse on your own and the problem just doesn't want to change, you might profit from a few therapy sessions. Couples counseling or family mediation may assist resolve brawls and teach skills for potential dispute resolution. You will also profit from traveling solo if your companion doesn't want to go.

1. Note that shared respect and seeking a compromise that pleases all sides should be the focus of good negotiation skills, not 'winning' the debate or 'being correct.'

2. This doesn't function in every case, but often it helps to lock hands or remain physically close while you speak (if you're experiencing a disagreement in a marital relationship). This can inform you that you both care for each other and that you value each other in general.

3. Bear in mind that being respectful to the other party is crucial even though you do not like their behavior.

Chapter 9: Exercises for Overcoming Anxiety

Progressive Muscle Relaxation and Deep breathing exercises are one of the most effective ways to reduce anxiety instantly. These methods

also help you to better understand while anxiety is creeping up on you at the moment. The fun part is that you can perform them anywhere or anytime without much effort once you have practiced the techniques a few times.

6.1 Progressive Muscle Relaxation

Progressive muscle relaxation shows you a two-step method to calm your muscles. First, in your body, you routinely relax various muscle units, like your arms and back. Next, as you loosen them, you relieve the stiffness and note how the muscles feel. This physical activity can help you reduce your average levels of stress and tension, and help you calm when you feel nervous. As well as optimizing the sleep, it will also help alleviate physical symptoms such as stomach problems and migraines. Individuals with anxiety issues sometimes become so nervous all day long that they don't really know what it looks like to be calm. You may learn to differentiate between the emotions of a stressed muscle and a fully calm muscle by practice. And, with the first hint of the muscle stiffness that follows the feelings of distress, you will start to "trigger" this calm condition. You understand not only what calm feels like by tensing and relaxing, but also to know anytime throughout the day you are beginning to get nervous.

Put some 15 minutes apart to complete the workout. Find a position without being interrupted where you can accomplish this workout. Practice this activity twice a day for the first few weeks, before you have the feel of it. The stronger you get at it, the sooner you can "push-in" the calming answer when you really need it! When you perform this workout, you do not need to feel nervous. Usually, when you are relaxed, it is easier to first do it. The way getting nervous can make things easier to do it.

Being Prepared

Find a peaceful, relaxed spot to sit down, then shut your eyes and let loosen your body. Great having a reclining armchair. You should lay down, but the risk of falling asleep would increase. While it will enhance your sleep by relaxing before bed, the purpose of the project is to learn to relax when awake. Carry casual, convenient clothes and do not hesitate to take your shoes off. Until you start, take about five long, deep breaths.

How to Do It

The Stress – Relieving Response

Phase ONE: Tension

The first move is to add muscle stress to one particular area of the body. This move is basically the same no matter which group of muscles you are addressing. Next, the emphasis, for instance, your left hand on the target muscle category. Then, for around 5 seconds, take a long, deep breath and contract the muscles as tightly as you can. It is necessary to really feel the muscle strain and may also create any pain or trembling. You will be forming a strong fist of the left hand in this case. It is possible to unintentionally tense other nearby muscles (such as the shoulder or arm), so aim only to tense the muscles you are focusing on Instead. With practice, it becomes simpler to separate muscle classes. Take caution not to injure yourself when your muscles are tight. While doing this workout, you should never experience extreme discomfort. Give the stress in the muscle deliberately and gently. Consult the doctor first whether you have trouble with pulled muscles, fractured bones, or other medical conditions that could impede the physical exercise.

Phase TWO: The Stressed Muscles Relax

This move requires accelerated relaxation of the tensed muscles. Let all of the tightness drains out of the stressed muscles after around 5 seconds. Exhale as you perform this move. When tension passes out, you can notice the muscles becoming relaxed and floppy. It is necessary to reflect on and note the difference between stress and relaxation quite carefully. The most significant aspect of the entire exercise is this. Learning to calm the body and note the difference between stress and relaxation will take time. It may feel awkward to concentrate on your body at first, but with time, this can become very relaxing. Remain for around 15 seconds in this comfortable condition, and then pass on to another muscle category. Repeat measures for tension-relaxation. Taking some time after finishing all of the muscle groups to appreciate the deep calming environment.

The Versatile Muscle Categories

You'll be interacting for nearly all of the big muscle units in your body through this workout. Begin from your feet and gradually step up (or if you like, you can do it in the opposite order, from your forehead down to your foot) to make things simpler to remember. Take, for example:

Foot (curl the toes in downward position)

Lower leg and foot (holding the calf muscle tight by bringing the toes into you)

Entire leg (squeeze the muscles of your thigh when performing the above)

(Reiterate on another body side)

Hand (fist clenched)

Whole right arm (stiffen your biceps by pulling your forearm up to your shoulder and forming a "muscle" when tensing your fist)

(Reiterate on another body side)

Buttocks (tighten the buttocks by bringing them together)

Chest (tightening by heavy breathing)

Stomach (sucking your belly in)

Neck and shoulders (raising back to hit the ears)

Eyes (clench your eyes firmly closed)

Mouth (open your mouth large enough to expand your jaw's hinges)

Forehead (raise your eyebrows to the maximum possible)

Listening to anyone who leads you to these measures will improve. There are several relaxing CDs for sale that can lead you to incremental (or anything quite similar) muscle relief. Likewise, on a cassette or CD, you might capture a script of this process, or ask a friend or relative to document it for you in a quiet, calming voice.

6.2 Deep Breathing

Breathing is a life requirement that normally happens without any consideration. Blood cells obtain oxygen while you take in the air and release carbon dioxide. Carbon dioxide is a waste product and is brought back and exhaled into the environment.

Wrongful breathing can disturb the exchange between oxygen and carbon dioxide and lead to anxiety, panic attacks, tiredness and other emotional and physical disorders1.

Breathing Reduces Anxiety

Most individuals are not particularly sure of how they breathe, but there are usually two forms of patterns of breathing:

1. Thoracic breathing (chest)

2. Diaphragmatic

As nervous people begin to take short, fast breaths that come straight from the chest. This method of respiration is called chest ventilation or thoracic ventilation. You might not even be conscious that you are breathing this way when you feel nervous.

Chest ventilation creates a disruption in the body's balance of oxygen and carbon dioxide, leading to elevated heart rate, dizziness, muscle pain, and other physical sensations.2 the blood is not oxygenated adequately, and this can indicate a reaction of stress that leads to fear and panic attacks.

You take deep breaths during abdominal/diaphragmatic breathing.

It's the way unborn babies breathe normally. When you are in a peaceful state of sleep, you're presumably just utilizing this method of breathing.

Chest vs. Abdominal breathing

The best way to assess your breathing rhythm is to position one hand in the center of your chest and the other on your upper abdomen close to the waist, and the other. Recognize which hand rises the most when you breathe.

If you breathe correctly, so the belly may move up and down with each breath. During a tense and uncomfortable moments where you're more apt to breathe through your chest, it's extremely crucial to be conscious of these variations.

Quick Respiratory Exercises

Try this easy calming strategy next time you're feeling anxious:

1. Via the nose, inhale steadily and profoundly. Maintain calm shoulders. Your belly should be rising, and very little of your chest should lift.

2. Exhale from your mouth, gently. Marginally purse your lips when you push air out, but leave your jaw loose. When you exhale, you can note a pleasant "whooshing" echo.

3. For some minutes, perform this breathing exercise.

As much as required, you may conduct this exercise. It may be done while standing, sitting down or lying down.

If you find this activity challenging or believe it causes you nervous or panicky, pause for now. In a day or two, do it again and progressively build up the time?

Often while performing this practice, individuals with a panic disorder briefly experience heightened fear or panic. This could be related to discomfort induced by concentrating on your breathing, or without any preparation, you may not be able to perform the exercise properly.

Conclusion

Healthy social experiences help us to handle our stressors, resolve disputes and resolve challenges properly.

There is all manner of partnerships that we have in our lives. Families, friends, bosses, neighbours and interpersonal and/or sexual experiences may be involved in this.

One of our most significant connection is towards ourselves. Before getting into intimate partnerships with others, it is important that we accept ourselves and esteem ourselves. This will set the groundwork for good, healthy partnerships with others if each spouse has a healthy sense of personal identity, self-esteem and adds to the relationship in a meaningful manner.

Society is highly influenced by what 'a good' relationship is labeled. Beliefs and practices concerning intimate relationships, marriage and sex differ widely around the globe, and in many societies, love is demonstrated differently.

Considering the human rights context, a healthy relationship requires our acknowledgment of our own feelings and values, as well as an appreciation of our partners' views, liberties and dignity. Several of the core aspects of successful relationships include unity, cooperation; honesty and accountability; mutual control; secure physical limits, good emotional limits, trust and caring, nurturing oneself. The first thing about establishing a successful and fulfilling relationship is that you accept people for who they are. Everybody has their own peculiar set of values, beliefs, expectations and memories, just like you. A healthy relationship is focused on commitment and entails all parties having honesty, harmony and mutual understanding, where each party is relaxed with the company of the other. Good relationships allow you to retain a grip over your personal life. Your partner should praise you for your wellbeing and for that. Without question, the most important element of a successful relationship is the mental wellbeing of all concerned. Get immediate help from a health professional when you suffer from tension, anxiety, insecurity or low self-esteem, and it is not just you, but also your families who would suffer.

You will not always withstand the stressors of your life, but strive to reduce stress to a minimum of order to be effective in your relationships. Also, when others step through a stressful time, be careful. For starters, for a while, someone who loses her or her job can behave cynically. Yet, life can eventually become simpler. "We just don't communicate!" It's a common refrain in relationships — may be too famous, since, after mental wellbeing, good communication is the second biggest aspect in a successful relationship.

CPSIA information can be obtained
at www.ICGtesting.com
Printed in the USA
BVHW091106090621
609092BV00003B/782

9 781892 507952